CELEBRATING THE MALE MYSTERIES

CELEBRATING THE MALE MYSTERIES

R. J. Stewart

AEON

First edition published in 1991 by
Arcania Press

Second edition published in 2022 by
Aeon Books

Copyright © 2022 by R. J. Stewart

The right of R. J. Stewart to be identified as the author of this work has been asserted in accordance with §§ 77 and 78 of the Copyright Design and Patents Act 1988.

All rights reserved. No part of this publication may be reproduced, stored in a retrieval system, or transmitted, in any form or by any means, electronic, mechanical, photocopying, recording, or otherwise, without the prior written permission of the publisher.

British Library Cataloguing in Publication Data

A C.I.P. for this book is available from the British Library

ISBN-13: 978-1-80152-009-6

Cover art by Cade Burkhammer

Typeset by Medlar Publishing Solutions Pvt Ltd, India
Printed in Great Britain

www.aeonbooks.co.uk

CONTENTS

PREFACE TO THE 2022 REVISED AND EXPANDED EDITION *vii*
PREFACE TO THE FIRST EDITION, 1990 (REVISED) *xiii*
INTRODUCTION *xix*

PART I: THE MALE MYSTERIES, ANCIENT AND MODERN
1. The god-within/-without 3
2. Men and the Goddess 21
3. Teachers and pupils 29
4. Polarity and sexuality 43

PART II: WARRIOR, POET, PROPHET, PRIEST, KING
5. Warrior, Poet, Prophet, Priest, King 55
6. The Worker and the Wheel of Life 79
7. The King within 87

PART III: VISUALIZATIONS AND EXERCISES
8. Visualizing transformation 97
9. Magic gods and visions 113
10. Empowerment and transformation 123
11. Toward the future of the Male Mysteries 153

APPENDIX 1: Approaching Silence 157
APPENDIX 2: Establishing an inner-world contact 161
APPENDIX 3: Visualization: the Guardian 167

BIBLIOGRAPHY 175
FURTHER READING 177
INDEX 179

PREFACE TO THE 2022 REVISED AND EXPANDED EDITION

This is an esoteric book, firmly founded within the Western Esoteric Tradition. It is about sacromagical skills and arts, not therapy. The book was originally commissioned by a small British press, long since passed away. I am pleased to offer it afresh, revised, to a new readership; some of the sacromagical concepts described in my original book, such as the male transformational cycle of Warrior, Poet, Priest, and Prophet appeared in later publications by other authors. The Male Mysteries are, of course, innate stages of male development and potential; they will stand through many explorations and expositions.

This 2022 edition has been substantially revised and expanded. It offers insights and techniques for the transformation of consciousness and associated energies, of vital forces. Certain Mystery traditions and teachings are included that had not been published before the first edition. As our culture changes with such speed, some of the purportedly secret methods of spiritual or sacromagical initiation have become obsolete, redundant. Yet others, long known but seldom taught, have come to the fore; a range of these are found in the practical exercises and forms in Part III. As I wrote in the original preface, on "How to use this book" (a sentence much loved by publishers back in the day), this is a book primarily for men, but I hope that women will also read it and try the practical exercises. The ongoing discussion on polarity and gender has been expanded for this edition. The way ahead is a shared way; let us all share it together.

Celebrating the Male Mysteries was written in 1989, and first published in 1991. To say that the world has changed in the three decades that have swept us into the 21st century would be a stunning understatement. The upsurge and ever-increasing domination and indoctrination of social media alone has created a different world to that in which the book was written.

As I write these words in 2021, the globally networked connected world is deeply divided and partisan over the endless comparison of fact and delusion. Whereas truth seemed just possible to grasp at the end of the 20th century, the 21st presents us with chimeras such as international hacking of government technology (often by other governments), "alternative facts," Q-Anon, and many far-ranging obsessive worldwide conspiracy theories. Such conspiracy theories would not be possible without the internet that miraculously and simultaneously provides us with both freedom of communication and creativity, and constriction of imagination and reason.*

*Lustig, Robert H. *The Hacking of the American Mind: The Science Behind The Corporate Takeover Of Our Bodies And Brains*, ISBN9781101982945

Men upon the couch

For our leisure, we are inundated with a plethora of technologically based fantasy entertainments with high energy impact; laser and strobe visuals and ponderous sound effects that were barely imagined in the 1990s and prior decades. There are, of course, many superb, thoughtful, beautiful, and educational productions that do not rely on superheroes and explosions.

Boys become men; men become boys. Old tribal ways toward male maturity have greatly diminished in the modern era, and hi-tech entertainment may simulate such ways, but cannot fully serve to replace them. We have yet to discover what will serve, but the methods offered in the later chapters of this book may go some way toward changing consciousness; as with all exercises, they will not work if we do not try them.

Nothing will be as it once was

Major concerns are growing due to the inevitability of rapid planetary heating and climate change; we will all be living within such changes for decades and then centuries yet to come. Planet Earth is a self-balancing homeostatic entity, and we are living in a time of increasing planetary adjustment. The time for serious work on human consciousness is now … without changes of consciousness we will not be able to embrace changes in planetary balance. The urgent message of the 21st century is this: *nothing will be as it once was*, and humanity can no longer hide from planetary responsibility. We are the planet; the planet and humanity are within one another, both physically and spiritually.

A global refugee crisis, the worst since the Second World War, is destabilizing nations and cultures, driven by conflict, staggering exploitation and hardship, disease and famine. As I write, the entire human population of Planet Earth is in the midst of the greatest pandemic for over a hundred years, perhaps the greatest ever. Suddenly many of the "normal" benefits of the modern world, such as the atmosphere-polluting wonder of international air travel, are, in effect, proscribed. Simple human joys such as eating in a restaurant with friends or family may risk potential infection and possible death; meanwhile, millions of humans can barely find food to eat. Thus the world of the 21st century is harsher, more at risk, and substantially more unstable than that of the late 20th.

Revisioning the Male Mysteries

Welcoming the opportunity to rewrite and present afresh the ideas in this book on the Male Mysteries, I found the task to be more than a simple reprint. I did not want to merely tweak a few edits, but to update many parts of the original book, cut some, and add new content. Most challenging was how to address the grim thought that compassionate spiritual progress seems to have ground to a halt under the immense pressures of our era; yet is this conclusion true?

The upsurge of the #MeToo movement and the revelations of ongoing concealed sexual abuse in the workplace, entertainment, church, and sports, has revealed to us all how entrenched and corrupt male stereotypes can be. Conspiracies are repeatedly exposed, crimes of sexual and authoritarian exploitation by certain men, of women, children, and younger fellow men. Perhaps the saddest truth is that we have not been surprised by the revelations, the cruel self-indulgence, and the moral bankruptcy of men in authority. This wave of revelations should make us all the more determined to bring male consciousness into a state of balance, beauty, and compassion.

The mystery of gender

Another significant issue for the 21st century is gender fluidity. Though it has existed for millenniums, it is regarded with suspicion, even hatred, by many who adhere to the Book Religions or live in the judgmental shadow of their influence. Gender fluidity and the wider range of LGBTQ awareness, was minimally addressed in the first edition, and I have attempted in this revision to explore some aspects of our currently contentious gender phenomena, from the perspective of the Male Mysteries and esoteric traditions. Yet gender fluidity, and bisexuality, were better known in the ancient world (the ancient Greeks, for example, acknowledged three gendered conditions, not merely two), and has always been known in the esoteric traditions. Magical practitioners have often led the way toward liberation from gender stereotypes, though the intense emotional and social dynamics and prejudices relating to male and female homosexuality, bisexuality, fluidity, and transition, are likely to be evolving for years yet to come.

Technology

The technology that is so all-consuming and potentially deleterious and addictive has been used fully and enthusiastically in creating this new edition. No more clunking groaning fan-roaring metal boxes vibrating at 16 megahertz (often under the desk thus unhealthily close to sensitive male genitals), no more behemoth radiation-blasting monitors (on the desktop thus unhealthily close to the face and brain); my computer is slim, silent, and portable. To begin the process of recreation, the first edition text of *Celebrating the Male Mysteries* was scanned into this sylph-like computer, a device that would have seemed astounding in the 1980s. Editing was achieved with sophisticated software, quite different from the old physical cut and paste process of wielding scissors, of spreading pages out on a table, cutting and rearranging them. Revision was assisted by the ability to instantly look up references on the internet, even while writing. No more traveling to reference

PREFACE TO THE 2022 REVISED AND EXPANDED EDITION

libraries ... journeys that I miss, as it happens; writers will do anything to have a pleasant day out and avoid writing.

Revisions, a kindly voice, and entering the Male Mysteries

The early chapters, 1–4 especially, have been revised in many places. Overall I felt that my voice of the 1990s should be modified to be more kindly, more supportive, less critical. Yet some would say we need an even more critical approach when relating to the tidal wave of illusion and the widespread flood of fake news through internet channels and social media. So pervasive is our tech culture that my writing software repeatedly replaced "modern" with "modem" during revisions. We do indeed live in *modem* times as much as *modern*.

The main chapters of the book describe in detail a series of methods, techniques, and hands-on practical work for changing consciousness, primarily male consciousness. As consciousness is ... well, consciousness, there is no exclusion of the feminine, only an emphasis on the masculine for the Male Mysteries. The techniques and their forms offer a contemporary way for men to initiate deep inner changes, using means that have stood for centuries within the esoteric traditions.

Sometimes the esoteric traditions have been so suppressed that they have gone underground, almost invisible, while in other centuries, such as our 20th and 21st, they have become increasingly visible and audible, in books, media, and a surge of both public and academic interest. Thus there was relatively little to revise (other than some tidying of language) in the later chapters, which, as we might expect, are the most significant part of the book. These chapters consist of visionary, meditative, and simple ritual *forms*, a term sometimes used for cohesive sets of training exercises in martial arts.

There are no matters of faith, belief, or superstition in the practical program offered here; try it, see if it works. Many people have found it to be effective over the last 30 years, and their experiences, as much as my own, have helped the evolution of the original book into this new edition.

I recommend that you read through the book first, as if it is a novel, before working seriously with the various exercises or forms.

The first edition was written in Bath, England, in 1989. This new edition was revised and expanded in Bath, West Virginia, 2021.

R. J. Stewart, 2021

PREFACE TO THE FIRST EDITION, 1990 (REVISED)

Authors note to the reader

This is a book on the Male Mysteries; I hope that both women and men will read it; however, the practical developments and exercises are specifically for men. It restates primal male magic through techniques for transforming consciousness and energy such as are found in humanity's perennial wisdom traditions.

In the chapters that follow there is a special emphasis upon our vast inheritance of such knowledge and techniques from Western sources, including those of ancient Greece, the Celts, Western magic and mysticism, and the wide range of primal sacromagical techniques found all over the broadly Western world. This is not a historical book but a practical one, and Part Three offers an original and unique working program of visualization for men, which has not been previously published.

I would not wish to be superficially accused of proposing any kind of return to outmoded male-dominated customs of social, political, religious, or sexual hierarchy: much of this book is intent on demolishing such hierarchies, and showing how deeply they damage us all, men and women alike. The exercises and illustrations are however, specifically designed for and about men, involving male energies and male responses to images in visualization. Thus, there may be an intentional absence of feminine aspects in some of the universal symbols used in the illustrations, such as the Wheel of Life or the Tree of Life, in which emphasis has been given to the male aspects.

Anyone who has read my books will know that they place a strong emphasis upon the feminine forces of the psyche (be they in a male or a female person) and upon the need for a continuing powerful ongoing revival of awareness of the Goddess. This awareness should be of nature, in humanity, of the universe itself, and without it we cannot reach balance, either individually or collectively. This book is a manual (no pun intended) for men who seek inner transformation, offering techniques that can lead to rapid and permanent results. There is however, both a specific and a running discussion of the relationship between modern men and the Goddess, and one of the deep levels of visualization in the work program involves powerful goddess images.

How to use this book

While writing this book, I have been aware of the difficulty that modern men may have in working with inner/spiritual matters, with the arts and disciplines of consciousness and energy. Not that we are incapable of doing so, but that many of us are unable to find what we think are the right personal or social circumstances to do so, and, of course, that simple information is often lacking. While there is a huge range of books and classes on both spiritual and psychological matters, there is less designed specifically for the man who seeks by inner means to transform and emerge into the future. Much of that specific knowledge has been denied to us by history and religion. This situation is explored more fully in the Introduction and following chapters of Part One, so I will take it no further here.

I offer a way of development by which the individual or a small group can work without feeling obliged to enter into existing movements, schools, societies, study groups, or any of the alternative mystical magical or psycho-therapeutic systems. What we must join are the inner Mysteries, not outer organizations. Both of my spiritual and sacromagical mentors in the 1970s emphasized that humanity is slowly outgrowing religious/spiritual/magical organizations; we need organisms of shared consciousness, developing relating and mutually evolving, to enable and accelerate that growth.

As the reader will soon discover, I feel that the way ahead for the Male Mysteries must come from a restatement and redevelopment of some of the primal male magic that has been hidden, suppressed, or perverted by vested interests over the centuries. Men have a habit of becoming over-zealous when they join movements or religions; the warrior urge and the religious urge are not that far apart from one another in men, no matter how much we might intellectualize or wish otherwise. Joining something—anything—often amplifies our weaknesses, giving us attractive and seductive excuses not to truly examine our motives and our deepest inner needs.

The practical work in this book, therefore, is designed either for the man working alone, or for a small group, possibly beginning from little or no experience of meditation and visualization. Having said this much, the exercises in Part Three are not simple tuition in such matters; with practice they emerge as powerful transformative tools, with many levels of possible effect. There are, of course, a vast number of handbooks on concentration and meditation, and some of these are listed in the Bibliography.

The key to development in the Male Mysteries is simple: calm regular work not upon but within one's self. The model of the Five Branches used in this book gives five categories of male energy and primal expression (Warrior, Poet, Priest, Prophet, King). These categories are well expressed in many publications as mythic or legendary themes, but the following chapters set out specific methods for working with them through a pattern of mutual interaction.

All Five Branches are inherent in each of us and have a further broad correlation to the human anatomy, subtle energies, and psyche. Arts exploring and expounding such correlation were a core aspect of the Mysteries, and later of Renaissance Hermeticism and Alchemy. While modern science regards these subtle yet intensely practical arts as outmoded, they still have much to offer if we are willing to work with them in an unprejudiced manner.

Empowerment and unity are found and developed within ourselves; we are the Primal Man, the Worker, the ruddy Adam in the Garden. As this simple fivefold model of male-being has resonances in us all, it is possible to develop exercises and visualizations which will be effective on progressively more powerful and transformative levels. In other words, the inner exercises and visualizations do not progress from beginner to advanced; this is the type of concept and potential delusion that men need to rid themselves of, as it so often implies meritocracy or divisive hierarchy.

A true hierarchy should also be a holism, in which all parts are integral to the whole and any part may be, paradoxically perhaps, the whole. The Five Branches model works in this manner and can be used by the man with no experience of inner arts and disciplines just as effectively as by one with years of training in visualization and meditation. The reader who is already familiar with some basic modern psychology will notice that the Five Branches used in our various forms are not the familiar mythic or family orientated archetypes, or life-phases so frequently found in modern publication and therapy. In this book you will not find extensive discussion of the roles of Father, Lover, Son, such as are often given in men's studies or groups, in psychology, and in revivals of esoteric or spiritual and magical arts today.

To a certain extent this non-emphasis upon such life-roles is organizational and intentional in the context of this book, simply to avoid confusion of methods and terminology. But upon a deeper level, the pattern of Five Branches used here, the male images and powers of Warrior, Poet, Prophet, Priest, and Primal Man or King, already have within each of them the archetypes or roles of Father, Lover, Son, and of course, the unifying role of Brother. Thus, the images or Branches may act and react as Companions or Brothers (a role which we concentrate upon in this method), Fathers, Sons or Lovers, just as any man may experience during his lifecycle.

Encounters

The deeper visualizations of the Mysteries involve encounters with Goddesses, who may act as Mothers, Lovers, and Sisters, yet often behave in other surprising ways. In this type of work, drawn from ancient traditions of empowerment, it seems to be the Companion, Sister, or Brother images (or gods and goddesses) that are required for modern work, prior to our real encounters with the universal Mother and Father images and energies. I would propose that this is a reflection of our current social and spiritual condition, in which there is a considerable imbalance between our male and female energies and modes of consciousness, and in which the collective and individual images of the Father and Mother are, as any psychologist will tell us, frequently corrupted and confused. In the mythology, religions and initiatory arts of the ancient world, however, we still find this role of the brother and sister deities specifically emphasized, and we see them acting to assist, enable, and transform humanity. In a purely male context, it is frequently the sister-goddesses who teach warrior and poet skills, inspire prophecy and priesthood, and both curse and bless certain heroes who epitomize humanity seeking to develop, transform, and become truly (rather than mechanistically or digitally) civilized.

Whatever is embodied in mythology may be activated through the imagination and will resonate in each and every one of us, male or female, if we do so. To restate and reopen the Male Mysteries, we need at certain stages to explore and experience the mythic patterns and powers described briefly above. For more detailed work with such patterns and powers, I will leave you to explore the visualizations and experiences offered in our later chapters.

There is an old Oriental saying that "when two masters meet, they smile". This has hidden depths. Initially it means that when two men well versed in their own spiritual traditions meet one another, there is joy and no antagonism between them. It can also mean recognition: the smile of recognition that comes when two men from traditions that may be culturally separated realize that they share the same experience, even though they have come to it by quite different routes. If you work well with the methods given in this book, you will eventually become liberated from any one tradition, religion, or set of beliefs, and will come to recognize spiritual presence and power when you meet it. Such power can often be in subtle guises, for good or ill.

The culmination of the exercises in Part Three of this book involves sequences of vision meditation and ceremony aligned to the Four Directions: East, South, West, and North. Through the Mysteries, a man unifies the world within himself, and brings together all directions harmoniously. Before he can do this, however, he must encounter the Goddess, the female forces of life consciousness and the universe, both within himself and in whatever outer expressions She may take in his life. Without this essential realization of the Goddess within, no man can find direction or begin to unify the Directions, and no society can be at peace, either with itself or with others upon the planet.

The first and last words of the Male Mysteries are those of the ancient encouragement, or some might say warning, written over entrance to the Temple: "Man, know thyself".

INTRODUCTION

The aim of this book is to present some insights and practical methods towards reinstating the Male Mysteries for the twenty-first century. The material presented is drawn mainly from perennial esoteric or magical traditions, utilizing practical methods which enable the individual to attune afresh to ancient and specific mythic and transformative potencies. We shall be examining some of these potencies, in the forms of energies, images, experiences, and thresholds of inner transformation in our later chapters. Many of the concepts and techniques are radically re-examined in a modern context, and some new methods, proven by long practice, are included.

The traditions upon which these new appraisals and techniques are based, however, are the enduring wisdom traditions, particularly those of Western magical and transformative schools of development. The nature and purpose of these schools or streams of tuition and initiation will be discussed in several places in this book, for there are many interconnected illusions and delusions, particularly in the realm of male spiritual development, that should and can be avoided.

What are the Mysteries?

Throughout this book the word Mysteries is used repeatedly. It is worth briefly defining how the word is used in our text, for there are several different meanings found in modern literature, and a quite distinct historical and cultural meaning for the Mysteries of classical and early civilizations.[1]

In a historical sense, the Mysteries of the ancient world were organizations that claimed to initiate members to levels of spiritual realization beyond those of regular temple or folk religion, or popular magical arts. They combined ceremony, imagery, fasting, meditation, instruction, and revelation. They were superseded and proscribed by the growing religion of Christianity, and eventually vanished as formal organizations.

Yet a number of underground movements and traditions have persisted right into the present century, albeit in attenuated forms. These manifested in each century in different ways and are often identified with certain "heretical" religious movements, magical or initiatory orders and societies, and the perennial collective teachings found within primal or folk traditions in every land. While we cannot say that any one of these many examples is a true Mystery in the classical sense, they are all representative of The Mysteries in a timeless sense, for they all combine many aspects of consciousness-changing techniques into certain loose formal groupings and traditions.

In this book the term Mysteries is used in the broadest possible context; it means any initiatory and instructional model of consciousness with sacromagical methods, as distinct from contemporary therapeutic approaches. Such streams of consciousness may have outer membership and meetings, or they may be accessed solely upon inner levels through meditation and visualization. They all begin where materialism, psychology, formal religion and common superstition falter and diminish.

The methods, potencies, traditions, images, and archetypes, employed in the Male Mysteries are shared by human consciousness worldwide, but manifest in varying forms according to culture, environment, genetics, and, of course, physical and metaphysical gender or sexual polarity. The entire subject of gender and consciousness has attracted increasing attention in recent years; much of this has been entirely divorced from the perennial traditions or wisdom teachings which, in their own remarkable way, deal extensively and profoundly with such matters.

Throughout this book we shall be discussing many topics relating to gender, and its physical and inner or metaphysical reflections, polarities, and potentials. There is a popular delusion that physical gender is unimportant in spiritual matters, or that we should 'rise above' sexuality in or through meditation and other spiritual disciplines. This delusion is one of the most enervating and poisonous traps for the individual, male or female, seeking liberation or enlightenment. Without an understanding of polarity, which is, of course, sexuality, our inner development or true balance simply cannot be achieved.

The very word "enlightenment" is dependent upon polarity, for we may not raise our consciousness at the expense of any "lower" part of ourselves or of others. Darkness is as essential to true psychic and spiritual realization as Light.

So many stereotypes regarding males as light-bringers and women as dark waiting wombs are found in spiritual literature and tuition, that it is sometimes difficult to grasp that such concepts play very little part in the inner spiritual teachings of our world. Such stereotypical roles derive from suppressive political religion, and though the originals from which they are corrupted are true and valid in themselves, the roles are only one fragment of a cycle of polarity: a fragment which can be dangerous if taken out of its deeper context. Fortunately, the spiritual and magical traditions worldwide have always shown how such cycles of polarity and balance arise, turn and return to their mysterious Source. This cycle, or more accurately spiral of cycles, is reflected in the Mysteries of every man and woman.

The influence of the Theosophical Society

During the middle part of the twentieth century, a powerful revival of the Women's Mysteries began, manifesting initially as a political movement. The feminist political movement, paradoxically perhaps, has some of its roots firmly in the convoluted esoteric and spiritual impetus of the Theosophical Society, whose great reformer Annie Besant worked unceasingly for women's rights in the nineteenth and early twentieth centuries. Enthusiasm for this Victorian and Edwardian politico-spiritual movement should be carefully tempered with a clear awareness of its powerful elitist and potentially suppressive hidden concepts. As it set the scene for the current revival of interest in spiritual matters outside orthodox religion, including the popular New Age movement we should briefly examine its role further. The Theosophical Society of today is a much- reduced organization that has abandoned many of its earlier precepts and clarified its core spiritual teachings.

The Theosophical Society, despite its many admirable achievements in the causes of womens' rights, racial equality, anti-vivisection, and the liberation of India from British rule, had a surprisingly wide range of elitist undertones, and for some years a neo-Messianic agenda. The much revised Theosophical Society of today has abandoned this agenda. Many of these undertones were also prevalent in other esoteric teachings and magical orders of the period, and some have persisted unbroken to the present day, often re-manifesting in the New Age movement. We shall touch upon such difficult and potentially suppressive streams of consciousness throughout this book, but for the moment state briefly the primary concerns that affect the spiritual growth of men.

The Theosophical Society, and related but far less politically influential magical Orders such as the Hermetic Order of the Golden Dawn, placed a strong emphasis upon Masters. These were an elite of supposedly superhuman males, living in secret isolation and dictating the progress of the human race. To a certain extent this concept derives from a perennial teaching concerning inner world or spiritual masters, who are said to exist in, and act or communicate from, other dimensions, and to relate to humanity in many varying but generally beneficial ways.[2]

The suggestion that such teachers are almost exclusively male, and that they are, in fact, super-physical beings moving secretly among humanity and steering our evolution, is a subtle but powerful twist to an age-old original teaching and has many negative ramifications.

Such concepts are anathema to spiritual development, to equality and harmony of the sexes, and to individual emotional and mental maturity. At the most juvenile level they can lead weak misguided men to assume that they are, or soon will be, such Masters but this is only the most obvious and trivial result. More subtly the concept of the Masters presupposes that humanity is little more than a series of manipulated races or, at best, a collective entity being steered by higher forces and specific (über-male) intelligences. The worst extremes of this type of occult teaching merge imperceptibly with racism and fascism, in which superior male immortals cultivate a racial elite at the expense of other "non-Aryan" or supposedly lesser races.

The hidden Masters today

Much of this negative dross has permeated through into certain modern or New Age cults and societies, that frequently claim wisdom and tuition from channelled sources, hidden Masters, and the advent of an elect or elite within the present or next century. This range of suppressive conceptual structures derives in turn from the political programming of historical or exoteric religion, carefully devised to generate belief in an Elect Few abandoning or even hostile to 'the damned', and firmly based upon male superiority. Chosen white men go to Heaven; women may follow obediently; the rest are insignificant and rejected.

Nor should we assume that movements based upon Eastern (or more usually, pseudo-Eastern) religions operating in the West are free of this long-term pernicious suppressive program; very often the veneer of Eastern spirituality and the glamorous use of exotic words and half-understood practices, masks what is at root an essentially Judaeo-Christian or Book Religion outlook. The much abused and misunderstand concept of karma is a typical example of this; another is the widespread loose use of terms like "higher consciousness" and "evolution" within esoteric, spiritual, and New Age teachings. When such terms are used, they frequently imply divisive dualism, leaving the material world of nature behind. We shall return to these subjects in our later pages, for both karma and evolution are central to the Male Mysteries, though not necessarily in the popularized manner in which they are often presented today.

None of this suppressive monosexual elitism is adequate or desirable for the twenty-first century, and the man or woman seeking inner growth should be very cautious indeed of working with any movement or set of teachings that derives from such sources or suggests such ideas. The most dangerous concepts are often subtly hidden or cunningly disguised with several layers of camouflage and are often only fully perceived through meditation and contemplation, rather than in an outer form, though such outer forms abound in the current expansive climate of alternative approaches to consciousness.

In our present context of the Male Mysteries, men need to be particularly aware that many lines or streams of concepts, of imagery, involving hidden Masters and so-called spiritual evolution, are in fact linked to the negative suppressive shadow of enlightenment, a word widely used to loosely mean spiritual liberation. For many centuries this shadow has resonated and manifested through male-elitism and male domination (of both primary sexes); such urging to dominate and suppress damages men as much as it does women. This is one of the major problems that men must address if they are to recover a proper Mystery or process of true enlightenment for the coming century.

Light darkness and shadow

Light is defined and enabled by darkness, and this mutual state of polarized existence holds good throughout all worlds, states, conditions, and cycles of existence. A shadow, however, is cast by all entities or shapes present within the light. Although we may not realize it, a shadow is defined and created only by objects present in light. Darkness absorbs all without distinction. There are no shadows in darkness: this is why the ancient Mysteries of Isis revealed the spiritual light of the Sun at Midnight, darkest of the dark, yet brilliant. This paradox is essential to the Male Mysteries.

At this introductory stage, however, we can consider briefly the existence of the converse or suppressive shadow of enlightenment, for it is not, and never has been, connected to antagonistic dualism between apparent good and opposing evil. The inner traditions—regardless of gender, race or creed—all teach that evil is a projection, confusion, or agglutination, of misaligned universal energy. It is not, as is so often propagandized within orthodox religions, an insoluble entity in conflict with spiritual qualities of goodness, to be combatted by formal religion.

The shadow of male domination is a resonance, a feed-back pattern of collective energies on many levels, ranging from physical through to psychic to metaphysical. If we are able to untangle and realign these corrupted self-perpetuating energies, we can make them available as sources of power which enable wholeness. The wholeness referred to is not only a psychological or therapeutic integration, but takes form within the pleroma or holism of the universe, mirrored through octaves or images such as the planet, the land, the harmony of races, and the individual human being, male or female.

The Gordian Knot

The late Robert Graves suggested that the legend of Alexander the Great (epitome of the powerful male stereotype), cutting the Gordian

Knot (emblem of the convolutions and weavings of the Mother Goddess) marked an important cultural and spiritual transition. Although Graves' writings have been used by modern pagans and followers of the Goddess in a manner which amused the poet himself, as his multi-facetted book *The White Goddess* contains many complex philosophical jests and poetic satires, we can pursue this particular image further. Only now are we discovering that the classical Greek world, the supposed model for Western culture, was not as we have been taught in class.[3]

The story of the Gordian Knot is one of the great classical allegorical legends and did not originate with Graves or any single writer scholar or poet. Like a number of mythic or legendary themes, the story of Alexander is full of emblems and images out of time; it is beyond yet rooted into history. Indeed, the cutting of the Gordian Knot is but one of many mythic themes that were gradually incorporated into the legends of Alexander. To amplify upon Graves' interpretation, we might consider that this event epitomized one of the symbolic thresholds, in mythic terms, between the older cycle of collective humanity worshipping the Goddess in her many presentations, and an increasingly male-dominated individualistic humanity. According to Graves and many other subsequent authors, male forces sought to control, through drastic divisive antagonist means, that which should in truth have remained whole.

Cutting a convoluted knot, which Alexander is said to have done to fulfill the prophecy that whoever loosed the Gordian knot would rule the then-known world, does not untangle it. The two parts remain as halves of an unsolved problem, now further divided by the sword, and thus doubly complex.

In a recent and still expanding revolution of awareness we have found that modern technology, one obvious example of divisive antagonist consciousness and energy manifesting into our world, has revealed to us its devastating planetary effect. Through science turning against itself at last, maturity begins to slowly dawn. We are collectively more aware of the terrible threshold upon which we stand: nothing less than the potential ruin of our planet as we know it. Even if we chop the knot or knots into the tiniest pieces, hacking away stereotypically and manfully and vigorously, we have still failed to untangle it. And besides, cutting a knot at the manifest level only disposes of that level, for its innermost subtle convolutions remain intact.

Modern Mysteries, male and female

The advent of open, or at least theoretically open, access to and practice of paganism in the post-war period has led to a large revival of Goddess awareness and worship in Western society. This shift of consciousness and revival of an ancient, but by no means extinct form of worship or holistic worldview, has been enthusiastically taken up by both men and women.

Men, however, have not had much open opportunity to reassess the inner or spiritual transformative dimensions of male potential. These were originally represented by what may be broadly termed the Male Mysteries in ancient cultures, and no counterpart of such systems or organizations exists today. Psychology frequently lays claim to techniques of maturation and integration which seem, quite plausibly and often with adequate proof and examples from case histories, to provide a path of development suitable for men. The twentieth century outburst of radical feminine awareness and Goddess consciousness is indicative of the failure of psychological techniques to meet the true need and power of the female psyche, either individually or collectively. The same failure is discovered in the context of male initiation, or inner development towards balance and full potential.

There is a considerable difference between a psychotherapeutic or psychological approach to male initiation and transformation, and that of the spiritual or magical traditions. Although psychology can find parallels between its own models and those of the esoteric traditions, such parallels only reach to a limited horizon. Beyond that horizon, the esoteric traditions extend, while psychology and psychotherapy must, due to their inherently materialist and limited nature, go no further.

In the 1960s there was a deep undercurrent of political and collective transformation of consciousness for women, much of which continues to ferment through Western society today. In the 1990s and 2000s this undercurrent touches men, initially from a psychotherapeutic standpoint, but ultimately as a re-evaluation and restatement of the inner magical and spiritual potentials of male entity. Beyond that, we must bring this potential out into the world at large, the world from which we can no longer artificially separate ourselves.

This book, however, does not take a psychological or anthropological approach. This is partly because these are amply represented in other publications and practical work, but mainly because the perennial traditions of spiritual and magical transformation, available equally and without distinction to both women and men, have a wealth of material concerning male inner transformation, most of which has never been published or reassessed for modern use.

Towards a new generation

During the 1970s and 1980s, a new generation of spiritual teachers for women began to arise. Such women have often come through political feminism, but have attuned to spiritual traditions, bringing new possibilities of transformation for women in general. In many cases these new possibilities are restatements of native traditions, rooted in a deep collective stream of awareness that regenerates itself in every century.[4] Can there be a new generation of teachers for men?

Before we can begin a proper answer to such an important question, we should dispose of some sentimental sweetness and light. Magnetic men with golden auras who exude loving brotherhood may, temporarily, give us inspiration during dark phases, but they themselves are often locked in a backwater from which they cannot or choose not to emerge. Traditionally the Male Mysteries, regardless of the culture in which they manifest or the form which they take, are just not that easy. Teachers in native or chthonic traditions, however, can be notoriously strict, devious, remorseless, or unkind.

We should carefully distinguish between this significant tradition of teaching in a non-sentimental manner—using perennial methods which aim to cut through all trivia and bring a true transformation within the pupil—and mere crudity or cruelty. The crude and cruel methods, perpetuated among men in barbaric ways even today, are founded upon ignorance. The ignorance within the male-superiority ethic; the necessary rigidity of the military mind; and, slightly more subtle but no less damaging, the delusion of meritocracy. The hard methods of spiritual and magical teaching, by comparison, are based upon deeper levels of understanding and wisdom, and have quite different goals, goals which might be incomprehensible to the man locked into seeking aggressive superiority. Only when a man is able to realize that such aggressive meritocratic aims are delusions, can he begin to truly mature.

For most of us this realization is present as an inner unrest, sometimes vague and too easily suppressed, but sometimes of such a demanding nature that it cannot be ignored. Suppressing and ignoring this realization of delusion leads to mental imbalance, to a reinforcement of the very traits that are the cause of our dissatisfaction. The vicious aggressive male ultimately destroys himself but can wreak terrible havoc upon others before he does so. Consider, in this context the dictators of the 20th and 21st centuries.

The transformations and realizations of the Mysteries are enabled by, and embedded within, techniques that have endured for millenniums, and have acquired a considerable collective energy and effect. We shall return to this concept.

We have all heard the suggestion and excuse that cruelty by teachers or parents is practiced "for his (or their) own good". Insecure bullying men have used this excuse for generations to allow themselves the thrill of imposing their will and physical strength upon younger men. This type of cruelty in training plays no part in the inner traditions. A wise teacher may often seem to treat a pupil in a harsh and uncompromising manner, in order to bring the pupil to a threshold of inner transformation. This does not, at any time, involve imposition of will and no one—male or female—can be forced into spiritual growth by another individual. The teacher may, and often does, create difficult situations or tasks which bring out the latent potential in the pupil. That is quite different to bullying. If we are to develop a new generation of men: men who will be able to pass spiritual perception and balance on to others, men who will forego egocentric inflation for the sake of a future society of harmony, we need to challenge many of the preconceptions of male dominated pseudo-spirituality.

The problem of the wise elder

The wise elder is a typical example of the problem of pseudo-spirituality. While many young men challenge and despise the false teachers of their childhood, rejecting those who imposed upon and indoctrinated them at school, very few of us challenge the root concept of the wise elder in its own right. We tend to accept that there must be (somewhere) older wiser men able and willing to teach young ones. Indeed, we tend to long for this type of teacher or leader, for not only is the delusion conditioned into us by our culture, but it plays heavily upon our weaknesses, our childish willingness to absolve ourselves of responsibility, and to pass all serious matters onto the shoulders of another. Not for nothing have the world's most vicious dictators been hailed by their people as saviors, fathers, holy men.

The true situation regarding teaching or mentorship is somewhat different. We all, men and women equally, learn most from interaction. In ordinary life this is, hopefully, acquired through experience, and we may have to undergo many bitter personal experiences before such interaction truly changes us. Through inner work in meditation, visualization, and other spiritual disciplines, we may slowly and thoughtfully dissolve the illusion of the stereotypical wise elder, and come to accept each teacher, inner or outer, simply for the quality and intensity of interaction, exchange, and hopefully, transformation, that he or she might have to offer. Some of the typical polarities and scenarios are well represented in the Mysteries, in mythology, in legend, and in esoteric training. Some are amply defined by modern psychology, though there is a tendency to limit the material to preconditioned and predefined interpretations.

Psychology and spiritual traditions

During the 1989 Merlin Conference, held in London, an open debate was engaged, based upon a motion that psychology has, effectively, stolen a fragment from the spiritual traditions known worldwide. Much of this debate is developed by a group of contributors in *Psychology and Spiritual Traditions* (Element Books, 1991), but as psychology is still a male dominated and male orientated field, it is worth some attention here, in the context of the Male Mysteries.

Psychology, regardless of any particular school or movement, is merely a model or concatenation of models of the human psyche. It may have little validity other than as a model, and the different schools of psychological theory and practice can and do disagree with one another. One of the problems of psychology is that it was developed almost exclusively by Western males without reference to alternative world traditions which contain other, often comprehensive, models of the human psyche.

Psychology has become an alternative to religion, an alternative to inner discipline and spiritual development. It has a difficult inheritance from the nineteenth century, when male intellectual giants were attempting to reach beyond religion and superstition; yet they were doing so in a society which was utterly conditioned by male-dominated religious conventions, behavior, beliefs, and attitudes of life. It was certainly a great achievement or a failure of the bootstrap theory, depending on your point of view.

Students and authors frequently cite C. G. Jung[5] as being a bridge between spiritual traditions and materialist psychology, but his role is really that of an Autolycus, a clever snapper-up of unconsidered trifles. Fragments of eastern and western tradition have been loosely incorporated into Jungian, and then into post-Jungian psychology, often out of their proper life-context or cultural traditions, merely because they are found to be effective in some respects and can fit into the framework of the psychological system concerned. Those aspects of the same traditions that do not fit, however, are conveniently ignored. Modern psychological techniques now abound, many of them claiming to be heralds of a New Age, to be transpersonal, to restate spiritual truths for the modern man and woman.

If we look closely at such alternative therapies, they are often based upon a small number of very simple and effective techniques which originally formed a part, and only a part, of broader traditions of spiritual and magical transformation. Frequently the result of taking such fragments out of their deeper original context is that they can become sources of imbalance, addiction to transient adjustment, or even a cult-like pseudo-religious obsession.

Typical examples, selected at random, might be as follows: primal screaming, rebirthing, encounter groups, psychosynthesis. These and other therapies all work; no one would deny their effect, yet they are fragments of techniques, either rediscovered in a vacuum, or deliberately borrowed from older traditions of transformation. Rebirthing, for example, is a commercially orientated reworking of the extremely ancient birth and incubation techniques known to the classical and Celtic cultures. Apart from this important but conveniently ignored connection to a fragment of the ancient temple techniques of past civilizations, rebirthing techniques are still practiced today among primal peoples for spiritual and magical initiation. Note that they are used for tribal or family initiation, and not for commercial therapy.

Many of the highly praised or advertised effects of alternative therapies, or of mainstream psychotherapy, are regarded within the magical and spiritual traditions as relatively minor results. In a modern therapeutic context, the catharsis of rebirth or of sudden realization is held to be an aim in itself; in the perennial traditions such events were merely part of a series of thresholds leading to inner transformation.

They were never ends in themselves, merely side-effects or transitional stages through which the individual passed on way to further change.

Labelling the problem

In more customary and conservative fields of materialist psychology, we still find the typical Victorian concern for labeling, from the years when psychology struggled to be recognized as a science. If something can be labeled, it can be ratified, but need not be understood. A label also distances us from the subject matter; we need not be involved in it too deeply, we can stand aside and consider it dispassionately; when we find something that we do not understand, something that instills fear, doubt or uncertainty, we try to fit it to our set of labels. Thus archetypes, gods and goddesses, mythic patterns, and the flow of energy in the human psyche and body, can all be reduced to a set of labels within a conceptual framework. We have a comfortable feeling, thereafter, of knowing what we are talking about, writing about, experiencing, or, perhaps, avoiding experiencing. Victorian psychology and occultism share this entrenched attitude.

The same concern with naming names is true of a Westernized approach to genuine ancient and contemporary magical and spiritual traditions; interpretations of the Mysteries (in any form worldwide) are replete with systems, labels, connective structures and so forth. But in practice they do not regard the system, the label, as being of any value in itself; there is no reductionism in the Mysteries unless the individual chooses, in a typical modern sense, to reach no further than the labels themselves.

This apparent similarity between mythic retellings, and obsessive textual listings is brought into proper focus when we realize that mythic epics and magical correspondences were not originally written down, but were vehicles of living oral tradition. The use of images and verses from memory rather than from the printed page is an essential aid to transformation of consciousness: this is why magical traditions insist on learning by heart what seems, to the modern intellect, to be a mass of superficially indigestible lore.

Much of our response to ancient mythic patterns and magical or religious systems is heavily conditioned by that same Victorian labeling as materialist psychology; it is most unlikely that the lists of correspondences used in the esoteric traditions were ever regarded as 'scientific' or 'authoritative' in the nineteenth century sense that still dominates much of modern thought and practice. They were more in the nature of incantations, dream flows, protean collections that were used to attune the consciousness to holistic models, rather than to reduce perception to an orderly checklist of items.

The Male Mysteries, like any branch of esoteric tradition, are essentially practical. The male-dominated elitist secret societies and occult orders of the 19th century, tended towards the intellectual, the hierarchical, and of course towards extreme obscurity. But there are older traditions, sometimes hidden within intellectual occultism and sometimes quite separate from it. It is the hidden traditions that we should restore and develop for the present day, and it is in those traditions that we find the direct teachings, myths and legends described herein as the Five Branches, with their empowering gods and goddess forms. And yes, there are some old-style lists of attributes in our practical exercises in Part Three. They are there so that after use, they can be reduced to healthy compost, rather than stand as sole definitions.

Part One explores the concepts of the gods within and without, and how men may relate to the overall concept and powerful presence of the goddess. The dynamic of teacher/pupil is examined, and perhaps the most essential for the Male Mysteries of our era: Polarity and Sexuality.

In Part Two we will examine the Five Branches of Warrior, Poet, Prophet, Priest, and King, and their effect upon the Worker or Primal Man who is both the beginning and end of the Mystery.

In Part Three we will use exercises in meditation and imagination that put us into direct contact with the god and goddess forms that empower each Branch, and we will develop a set of simple but powerful methods of working with such images for individual and group transformation and empowerment.

PART I

THE MALE MYSTERIES, ANCIENT AND MODERN

CHAPTER 1

The god-within/-without

Men and the God

So many confused, contradictory, and interlaced assumptions have been made about the relationship of men to gods, the god, God, that it would be a huge task to untangle the resulting complex mess. Perhaps we do not need to untangle it, as much of it is already rotten and being discarded. In our present context of Male Mysteries, we do not need to delve deeply into the dogma of formal religion; instead, we can work upon a subtle esoteric level that both transcends and underpins many aspects of religion, psychology, and inner or transpersonal development.

There is no elitism in this book, only the suggestion that men can learn directly from perennial educational initiatory traditions. Such wisdom traditions reveal the essentials behind magic, religion, and myth. These essentials are surprisingly simple, though they have often been presented in a complex manner. They are obscured by an accumulation of arts, sciences, and religions in each century. Modern developments of the Mysteries do not demand religious faith, nor do they deny it. The concepts and resulting exercises in this book are of a practical and technical nature; they can be practiced and experienced and are based on techniques that have long been known in the Western Esoteric Traditions. They require willingness more than obedience, discipline more than faith, and wonder more than dogma.

Of more concern, however, than any fruitless argument over the validity of dogma or faith, are the long-term psychic and social effects of such dogma and of spiritual suppression. These long-term effects have worked deeply upon both men and women, and on this collective and individual level clearly the relationship between males and the god is in a very sorry state indeed. Nor has modern psychology been helpful to us, especially those branches of Jungian and post-Jungian psychology, which seem to take a great interest in mythology and perennial imagery. Although some schools of psychology are considered to be amicable and even helpful toward spiritual realization, they may ultimately be more confusing in effect than the excesses of behaviorism or hardline Freudian theory and practice, both of which mostly leave the perennial wisdom traditions alone. Jungian, post-Jungian, and transpersonal psychology is all too frequently limited to those segments of ancient wisdom, magic, and mythology that fit a theory, while blandly discarding or ignoring those (by far the greater part) which do not.

Much emphasis has been placed by psychology and psychotherapy upon masculine and feminine qualities of the psyche, which are said to make themselves known through archetypes or god-forms, often those defined in ancient myth. These psychological archetypes (the word archetype is used in psychology with a derivative meaning different from its original in ancient philosophy) are assumed to be fragments or resonances of either a collective or an individual psychic state, as aspects of consciousness. But they are not considered to be aspects of any ubiquitous transcendent, universal consciousness, or, for want of a better term, Divine Being. The original meaning of archetype has been adapted into a materialist role.

When psychology deals with the gods, the gods do not exist in their own right; they have no relationship to any universal holism or existence beyond the human psyche. There are many subtle implications to this type of theory, not the least of which is that any empowering concept or potential experience of either god or goddess may be undermined by suggestions that it is nothing more than the projection of a psychic construct, psychological archetype, or sub-personality. Nothing could be further from the ancient concept of the goddesses or gods. The aim of developing a modern Male Mystery is to discover how men might interact with the spiritual dimensions as fact. Not through faith, belief, or therapy, but through expanding experience.

The god-within and -without

We may begin by considering the god-within. What is this notion of a divinity inherent in humanity? Why do we feel, through all ages and cultures, that there is something inherent in every man that pertains to a god or gods, and in every woman that pertains to a goddess or goddesses? And in all men and women, regardless of gender or sexual preference, an androgynous core of Being that both transcends and underpins our transient individual expressions as human beings.

In the Male Mysteries, one of the major empowering techniques and experiences is to realize the presence of both the god-within, and the god-without. There is an unfortunate tendency for the concept of the god-without to be used for religious suppression of individual freedom, and for the concept of the god-within to lead to egotistic inflation and, in some cases, to the extreme evils of scientific materialism, the abuse of life, and the destruction of the environment. As we have discovered, with growing certainty in the 21st century, the hubris of materialist science, striving ever onwards and seeking to wrest secrets from nature, linked to a profit motive where anything is allowable to "make a dollar," has led directly to the wasting of our planet. We will be paying the true price, the irreplaceable value, for many years to come. Scientists tend to pass the blame to corporate interests, who tend to pass the blame to governments. Someone, somewhere, is responsible.[6]

We might not think such gross imbalances and obsessions are directly related to the god-within … but materialist indifference and arrogance is part of that awareness of potential divinity; we behave like ego-maniacal infants with powerful toys, knowing at last that there is no chiding deity to punish us for our so-called sins. Materialism is the direct result of Christianity within imperial history; the religion that declared nature not to be sacred, but to be evil and therefore legitimate to abuse. This justification of the abuse of nature and all other entities, including non-conforming humans, is at the heart of the Book Religions, as much as at the heart of materialism and scientism.

We are not solely concerned here with negative manifestations, but rather to seek a balanced insight into the simplest roots and energies that comprise the relationship between a male human and the empowering entity or energy of a god. At this stage, it is irrelevant what name, kind, type, or origin the god may or may not have. If we were to strip the entire subject of both religious and psychological jargon, we would find a very simple set of concepts, a situation that can be accepted or rejected. If we accept these concepts, or, more importantly, if our intuition and meditations confirm that there is truth in them, they act not only as a foundation for establishing parameters of consciousness and energy but as initiatory thresholds toward inner change. This is what the Male Mysteries, and indeed any Mystery or structured system of revelation catalysis and inner change, are all about.

Gender and polarity

The male entity, defined generally but not exclusively by gender, is the human biological equivalent of a universal relatively male or positive polarity. The female entity is relatively negative in polarity. The relationship between positive and negative is fraught with dualistic, deeply ingrained value judgments when it comes to defining and working with consciousness.

By the terms positive and negative, we emphatically must not imply good and bad, or any illusory fixed value whatsoever, but should simply define relative polarities of energy.

Such polarities cause movements of energy and form, which arise, cycle, and transform through an infinite number of states or conditions in our universe. The relative divisions or interactions are simply a property of consciousness in time, our way of filtering the holism into smaller archetypes or sub-sets to which we can relate. In altered consciousness, different from our habitual or conditioned state, hitherto unrecognized, resonances or octaves of the universal holism are perceived and experienced.

In the human physical body, our sexual definition is that of the penis and vulva (the first being physically outreaching; the second being physically receptive). But upon inner levels of energy the esoteric traditions (regardless of culture) teach that the male can be sexually negative or receptive, while the female can be sexually positive or outreaching: the polarity cycle is ever-spiraling. This teaching has been known for thousands of years in the magical arts, yet has been heavily suppressed by orthodox religion and related social and political expressions in our culture. It lies at the very heart of powerful sexual or polarity magic in which energies are exchanged, transformed, and greatly amplified through the flow between the alternative polarities of the humans working the magic, visualization, or ceremonial pattern. This "secret" dissolves the rigid dogma and social conditioning regarding male and female, and flows through all matters not only of gender, but of sexual orientation and preference.

Esoteric tradition uses a number of simple but profound conceptual models to show this subject of cyclic polarity, and to relate them within a holism that ultimately resonates through all Being. Typical examples of such models are shown in Figures 1 and 2, The Wheel of Life and The Tree of Life.

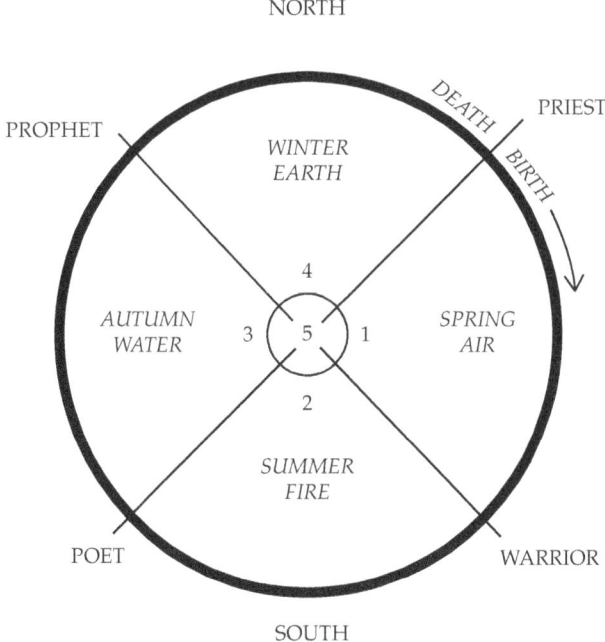

Figure 1: The Wheel of Life.

The Wheel of Life is a map, glyph, or mandala showing four fundamental relative states of energy, consciousness, and being. They interact as four ideal Elements of AIR/FIRE/WATER/EARTH, and as the Four Seasons of SPRING/ SUMMER/AUTUMN/WINTER. In meditational work they are aligned to Sacred Space (see Figure 10), the Four Directions of EAST/ SOUTH/WEST/NORTH, and the Quarters of the day, DAWN/NOON/ EVENING/NIGHT. Work within this fourfold pattern leads to harmony, relatedness, balance and rhythm.

Our life-phases of CHILDHOOD/ADULTHOOD/MATURITY/AGE reflect the Quarters of the wheel or compass, with further rhythmic connections to the Lunar cycle of Waxing, Full, Waning, and Dark Moons (see Figure 7). The relative fourfold cycle is inherent in every energy pattern, every being. If we work from the still center of the Wheel rather than repeatedly spin around it, we enter into a deeper understanding and conscious realization of all aspects of the Four Quarters.

In the Male Mysteries, this consciousness is embodied as Four Companions the Warrior, Poet, Priest, and Prophet, who stand at the intersections of the Quarters, Elements, and Seasons. They are inherent in every man, but are brought into consciousness through meditation, visualization, movement, and rhythmic work within the Fourfold Circle.

The flat pattern of the Wheel or Circle is really a map of our spherical field of energy/consciousness. It is completed and brought alive by a human being in its center, through the Directions of Above, Within, and Below. This is shown in Figure 10, defining Sacred Space.

The Wheel of Life is also the ground plan for the primal universe, perfect world, idealized state, spiritual city, and the balanced sacred land. Such fourfold zones were frequently used in ancient cultures to attune the physical land, bringing a deep sense of relatedness and cyclic energy between humans and the environment.

1 = Childhood/Dawn (0–20 years)
2 = Adulthood/Mid-day (20–40 years)
3 = Maturity/Evening (40–60 years)
4 = Age/Night (60–80 years)
5 = Center of Being (timeless presence)

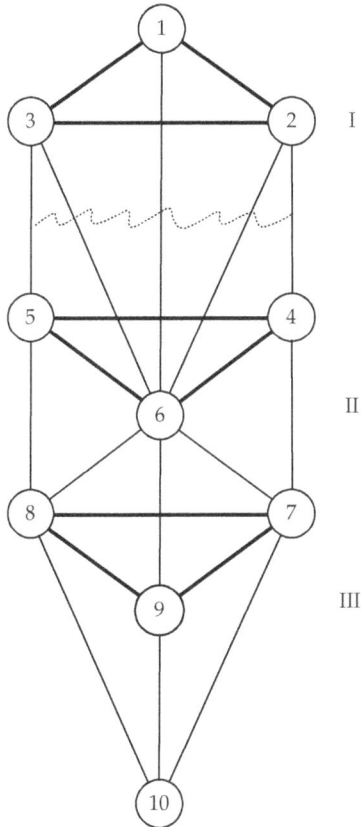

Figure 2: The Tree of Life.
Note: I Stellar World, II Solar World, III Lunar and Earth World.

The Tree of Life is a traditional image combining human, planetary, mythic, and energetic attributes into a harmonious structure. It is used in various presentations in meditation and visualization, and has a close correspondence to the energy centers of the human body. The Tree or Axis Mundi (World Pillar) grows in the center of the Wheel or Sphere of Life (see Figure 1). This empowers our perception of Sacred Space with an idealized model of the Cosmos. The universal image of the Tree comprises Earth, Moon, Sun, and Stars as a central pivot, the planets and stars as polarized energies to the right and left, and the relative directions of the universe defined as Four Powers inherent in all being: LIFE/LIGHT/LOVE/ LAW (ESWN).

Ultimately, the Tree of Life and the standing human, the individual at the center of the Circle or Wheel, are unified. In the Male Mysteries this is the realization and manifestation of inner balance or Kingship (see Figure 6).

The Tree of Life comprises three triads or reflections of polarized male/female energy, each having a correspondence to the human body, which reflects universal patterns and energies within itself. The first triad is stellar or universal, the second is solar or planetary, while the third is Lunar and of our Planet Earth. These are frequently shown in three concentric circles. The ten polarized spheres of the Tree are:

1. *Crown (of head): Primum Mobile or originative Universal Being. Inspiration, breath, passes out and in through the throat.*
2. *Wisdom (left shoulder): The Zodiac or stellar wheel. Stellar gods, or the Star Father.*
3. *Understanding (right shoulder): Saturn. The Great Mother.*
4. *Compassion (left arm and side): Jupiter. Powers of Giving or creation.*
5. *Severity (right arm and side): Mars. Powers of Taking or destruction.*
6. *Harmony (center/heart): Sun. Powers of balance, centrality, beauty.*
7. *Victory (left): Venus. Emotions or soul.*
8. *Honor (right): Mercury. Thoughts or mind.*
9. *Foundation (center/genitals): Sexual and fertility powers.*
10. *Kingdom (feet): Matter, the manifest body, powers of the planet.*

Polarity Patterns: The energies of 1/6/9/10 are central and bisexual, 2/4/8 tend to be embodied by male beings or deities, 3/5/7 tend to be embodied by female beings or deities. It is possible to define variants of the Tree of Life that emphasize either gods or goddesses in mythic terms.

The basic condition of maleness (as distinct from masculinity) is defined by but not limited to physical gender. This can mean that when various life energies manifest upon the physical level, they tend toward a positive or male polarity. Upon inner levels, which are reached through imagination, visualization, meditation, and (less frequently but very effectively) through ritual or ceremonial patterns, the polarity or energy flow will change many times. Each threshold or change reflects an inverse: that which was immediately male upon the physical level becomes female inwardly then crosses another inner threshold and becomes male again. This interchange offers many insights into contemporary issues of gender fluidity and transition.

From an esoteric perspective, the deeply felt changes come not from a personal source seeking manifestation, but a spiritual source, resonating outward from the inner or metaphysical dimensions, through the psyche and physical body. The Tree of Life offers many insights on this, in meditation.

Much of this sequence is shown in Figure 3—Polarity Thresholds.

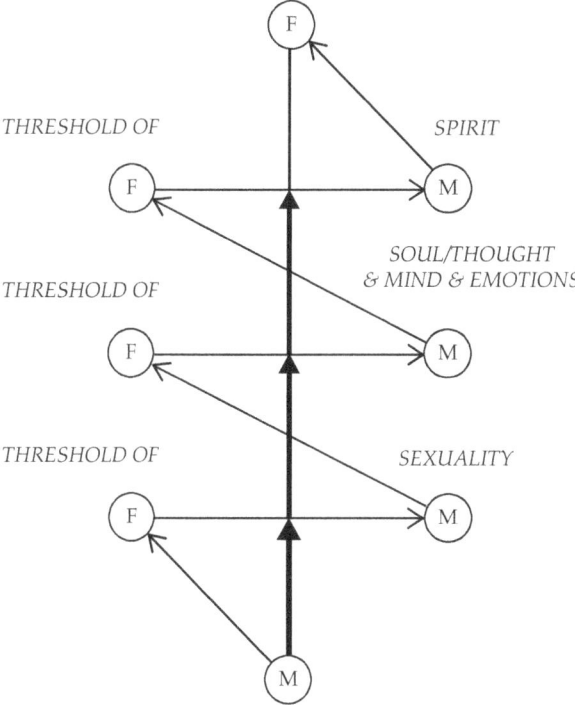

Figure 3: Polarity thresholds.

All human beings are bisexual or potentially balanced and androgynous, regardless of physical sexual definition. Many of the stereotypes of masculinity and femininity vanish in meditation and visualization with the discovery that gender does not define consciousness. Three main thresholds are often found in meditation or conscious work with inner energies and at each threshold there is an initial reversal of polarity:

1. *Outward male body/First threshold of sexuality/inner female energies. Re-polarizes as male prior to:*

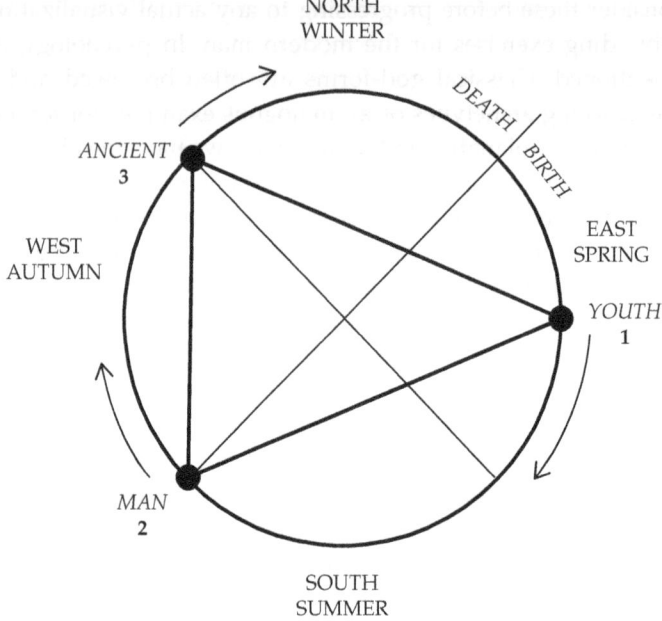

Figure 4: The Three Faces (youth, man, ancient).

Another way of relating male energies and images to the Four Elements, Directions, and life cycle, is through a triple pattern. This is frequently found in mythic images of gods and goddesses throughout the world. Any god or goddess image or archetype may appear in any of the Three Phases, youth, adult, ancient.

A full cycle around the Wheel of Life (see Figure 1) will generate 12 images, god-forms, or archetypes. These may be embodied as mythic beings or as constructs within the psyche appearing in dreams, waking images, and as spontaneous figures arising in visualization. They may also arise in primal or shamanistic arts as ancestral beings, which will often occur in triple presentation, with different implications or teachings according to the phase of youth, man, or ancient.

The triads of Figure 2 and the cyclic and fivefold shapes of Figures 5 and 6 can be related to this triangular shape in meditation. The pentagonal shape of Figure 8 is derived from the heart of a hexagram, formed of two intersecting balanced triangles aligned to the Four Directions. These simple properties of shape and relative energies have powerful transformative effects when they are used in techniques of empowerment through meditation and visualization. They also play a major part in sacred dance or ritual pattern making, in which movements of our bodies in a defined space reiterate the energies and patterns of Sacred Space, of the universe.

At first this might seem to be merely a matter of chronology, and it certainly has its parallel in the human life cycle, but the Three Faces of a god (any god) tend to relate harmonically, or holistically, to certain properties and energies of consciousness: bright prophetic child or youth/wild or mad adult man/wise and experienced elder.

If we take Apollo as a typical example of these Three Phases, the stereotypical Classical Apollo, god of the Sun, of mental discipline, music, and intellect, is interpreted by 18th- and 19th-century preconceptions, deriving directly from male-dominated monotheism. In the 21st century, a number of academic writers, especially women, have exposed how subject to male religious prejudices our inheritance of Classical myth has been. If we look at the myths and geomantic locations of Apollo, and of his Celtic manifestation Mabon, and the Welsh/Scots medieval texts about the prophet Merlin, we will find a quite different pattern, relating to the Three Aspects described above.

Finding the god-within

As we have already suggested, the god may be found within or without. The god-without has, in broadly Christian cultures, for about 1,500 years, been increasingly and severely limited to a monosexual and imbalanced image, the "demon Jehovah" (as William Blake described it).

Thus we inherit the wrathful father, the creator of pain, suffering, inequality, restriction, elitism, misery, white domination, imperialism, and so forth. This terrible image has been mitigated slightly by that of Jesus, but suffering and pain are also features of this divine Son in most orthodox Christian cults or religious branches. The problem of rivalry and pain between father and son, or older and younger males, seems epitomized in the formal Book Religions. This unfortunate and destructive historical pattern, in which corruption of a mythic father/son divine pattern has heavily influenced human historical development, undermining the collective psyche and creating conditions of imbalance and effective evil, cannot be simply undone, even today during the incremental collapse of Christianity as a force in our world.

Nevertheless, a man seeking the god-without, outside himself, can still take the orthodox religious route, though it is fraught with terrible barriers and suppressive imagery. To reach the true level of divine love and compassion that was originally embodied within Jesus of Nazareth, a man may have to work his way through the entire ambience, collective imagery, and repressive forces of orthodox religion. He may well lose sight of his original goal en-route, or, as is more likely nowadays, simply realize that a corrupt and defunct religion is not worth his life energy. The failure of Christianity to meet the needs of modern people means that many individuals are lost, seeking a religious focus, but failing to find one. Too often, the active cults of Christianity that seek recruits are of such a repellent nature, lacking adequate compassion or spiritual wisdom, that many people are unable to accept what little they have to offer. None of this impacts the spiritual heart, the original compassionate and redemptive impetus of what eventually became called Christianity. The irony is that it can be best found outside the orthodox Churches.

What, therefore, are the ways in which a man finds the essential Being, the power, the divinity, within himself? In Chapter 3, we discuss some of the ways of action, skill and craft, and balanced living, which act as outlets or routes for the energy of life as it is expressed through a male identity. These are not offered as a so-called "authoritative" list, but are indicators drawn from sacromagical and spiritual teachings through the centuries.

Finding the god-within, the essence of our being, is related to sexuality. For many men the initial path is to work with a male-gendered self-image; that image is then modified and eventually abandoned, discovered to be the temporary mask that it truly is. But what does it mask? Energy, life-force, and within that energy a Being that is more than our assumed/conditioned selves. In terms of our own awareness, even when it is beyond the delusion of a rigid personal self, this higher or transpersonal entity, this being, is still recognized at first as male. Not One Being, which is before polarity, but a higher order of being that is before personality. Working consciously with Mystery techniques, building interactions with chosen deities, brings change.

At the most profound levels of meditation, such sexual identification vanishes, and the essence of Being is known to be androgynous, transcendent, yet totally present within all sexuality, all polarity, all time, space, and energy. The further we reach inside ourselves through meditation, the less defined sexual polarity becomes. In other words we do not intentionally pass within in meditation to be repeatedly confronted by superior male fragments of ourselves: we pass beyond any such relatively surface levels, and seek directly for the deeper roots of our being ... this seeking will often, in itself, rebalance fragmented and habitual tendencies toward exaggerated stereotypical habits and behavior.

Many men are afraid, even terrified, of any type of inward-looking meditation. They tend to confuse it, perhaps intentionally, with weakness, self-examination, or moody introspection. We may set aside, for the moment, obsessive self-examination, or ego-mirroring and self-reassuring reveries and daydreams ... these are not meditation, not true visualization, and they do not reach far beyond the more superficial levels of the psyche. In some men there is a highly energized loop of self-mirroring fantasies, such as perpetual self-examination, dwelling upon one's own thoughts, emotions, motives, decisions, and so forth. Another typical and widespread self-mirroring fantasy that rules the lives of many men is the delusion of the man's man, the praise-greedy narcissistic phallic erect achieving male. In recent years the USA endured a shockingly destructive president who epitomized such narcissistic delusions to a high degree.

In Britain, the Medallion Man, who looks in every mirror, wears his shirts open to reveal his medallion, became a familiar figure of comedy and ridicule. And let us be honest at this point, we have all behaved, at some time, somewhat like Medallion Men. This type of self-image runs through many male activities and occupations; so many men have little concept of what they truly are, whom they are, relying instead upon a mirror built of stereotypes of pseudo-manliness. Such stereotypes are deeply embedded in our culture, strongly supported by advertising and social media, and entrenched in workplace culture.

The god-within is not a type of phallic super-male, nor is it the function of the god-within to release energies that might enable us to behave badly, in a manner that amplifies and encourages our current habits and delusions. One typical problem is that when men encounter their innate power within, either through an early meditational or spontaneous experience (such early experiences can be very potent indeed), or through involuntary realizations (which come to all of us at least once in a lifetime), or through unusually highlighted or tragic circumstances which lead to a sudden change of consciousness, they tend to re-route

CHAPTER 2

Men and the Goddess

Just as it is impossible for women to truly realize balance and maturity without an open relationship with their inner male energies and responsive psychic entities (the god-within), so is it impossible for men to gain such realizations without their inner female energies and psychic entities (the goddess-within). Psychology has gone some way toward recognizing and discovering this truth, which was widely taught in the ancient Mysteries, and has persisted, often in rather obscure presentations, in the perennial esoteric traditions.

A degree of insight into the truth of the god- and goddess-within is only the first glimpse or reflection of a greater picture, for both men and women should also establish a proper relationship with, and within, the Great Goddess.[7] She reflects through our inner energies, but She is a universal power and entity, a Being directly from the One Being, underpinning, permeating, and transcending all other forms and forces.

No energy or space will be spent in this book discussing or trying to prove the existence of the Goddess; this is not a treatise on philosophy or religion. Exercises that include working with Goddess power will more than prove her reality to even the most rigid and skeptical male, if he is prepared to work with them. The effects of such exercises, of course, will vary considerably, and some of the possible range of reactions will be outlined in various contexts throughout our later chapters. As this is a book on the male potential for enablement and transformation through esoteric initiatory techniques, the range of reactions described is broadly confined to those found within men, but they mirror those of women in many ways.

None of the foregoing implies that all women have an inherent natural relationship with the Goddess, any more than it implies that all men have a natural relationship with the God. Many may not. One of the false assumptions in contemporary methods, teachings, and practices is that physical gender gives an individual some kind of spiritual entitlement ... that women must, because of their gender, be in contact with the Goddess, and likewise men with the God. This can become a trap that often runs through esoteric groups and magical orders today. It is really a type of subtle sexism, of gender stereotyping, and can cause ongoing damage to spiritual development by placing unnecessary assumptions and expectations within the individual psyche. If I am a Man, why does the God not come? If I am a Woman, where is the Goddess? They are always there for you, but you must meet them halfway.

In this context we have ample evidence from literature and iconography that in the pagan religions it was common for women to mediate, invoke, and act as priestesses of gods, while men performed the same functions as priests of goddesses.

One of the more curious aspects of the modern revival of Paganism and Goddess worship is that it often seems to fall into the sexual stereotype trap that has such a grip upon Christianity, though it manifests in a more subtle way, as we might expect. Because for many centuries no one had dared to say publicly that the Goddess lives within women, this statement is now assumed to be inevitably true, possibly through its shock value to those conditioned to patriarchal stereotypes of religion. We should also remember that it was generally heretical and punishable for men to state that the God lived within them; God was always safely outside, usually upward, and strictly regulated by dogma, to be contacted solely through authoritarian bodies of priests, rabbis, and the like. Some magical groups and orders still perpetuate this sexual problem, in which only men are supposed to be able to mediate godforms or male energies, and only women can mediate goddesses. In the current period of increasing gender fluidity, this restrictive concept has caused some serious disputes and much anger from time to time among revival magical and pagan adherents.

However, gender-rigid suppositions are fundamentally untrue; historically, we may find many examples of polarity working within sacerdotal and magical practices (i.e., males relating to goddesses and females to gods). This historical evidence is borne out very powerfully indeed in modern experience and practice of magical arts and esoteric techniques. Some men may be deeply shocked by the suggestion that they can relate directly to the Goddess, or act as her priest—and little wonder after such a long period of deliberate suppression of this great truth.

In our context of the Male Mysteries we are concerned mainly with the transformative potential of the inner energies upon and through men, but it must be emphasized that men and women are originally ultimately and potentially bisexual; a balanced humanity is one in which women and men are equal. A number of myths and legends demonstrate this truth, often with several levels of meaning.

In our current state of human development, balance may occur through male–female partnerships, but this important archetypical concept has been perverted and corrupted by dogma within the Book Religions, and further degraded by the subsequent entrenched stereotypes of our society. Our human potential of equality and balance, however, remains ever-present for us. It is often found upon non-physical sexual levels, and much confusion and emotional disablement arises when men confuse inner partnership with emotional or sexual attraction. (This confusion is one of several exploratory themes in Dion Fortune's early 20th-century novel *The Sea Priestess*)[8]

The root of this type of problem, increasingly common as more and more people turn to inner disciplines and practices, is that the general expectations of emotional relationships are widely at variance with the reality of our inner situation. One of the potential weaknesses of therapy is it may not address the deeper levels of polarity or spiritual sexuality, and can sometimes work against the true inner nature of the individual. Such enduring and widespread confusion over the emotions and sexual polarities is one of the true victories of the suppressive long-term programs seeded into human culture by manipulators of religion, destroying our potential for liberation, and amplifying imbalance and antagonism between men and women.

We shall return to this major subject in several respects, and in a number of variant forms and situations, as it arises in the context of the Five Branches of the Male Mysteries. Spiritual balance may also be of the universe, as inherently feminine. Not as an act of faith, not stereotypically feminine, not the yielding passive Earth abused by the capitalist profit-orientated polluter, plunderer or destroyer, not even the Earth Mother, though She is part of this holism. Those who are devout materialists can make such a change of awareness just as easily, possibly more easily, than those with some type of spiritual conviction or knowledge. The fact that it is a mental trick, an intentional change of attitude, in no way limits its remarkable effect. Try it for ten days ... or longer.

As with all such practices at first we slip away from our attention to it, but when we begin to feel it rather than think about it, to sense it in the body more so than in the abstract, it opens out. Steady repetition works well for such exercises, more so than determination and intense efforts at concentration.

For men, this transformation of perception is one way of developing a gradual realization of the Goddess; other ways, embedded within the wisdom traditions of the world, the Mysteries, are the cathartic and often devastating initiatory images of the Dark Mother, the Death Goddess, the Warrior Sister, all of which are essential in the Male Mysteries. If we resist these natural universal forces, they will eventually manifest through our outer lives. In the most obvious way, none of us can ignore physical death.

Mother and lover

Although we live in an era when it seems that a revival of Goddess-awareness is genuinely occurring, we should be alert to the pervasive presence of enervating stereotypes within this revival. In many examples, it seems only too clear that what people are reputedly reviving is a set of inflated artificial images, rather than a true relationship to the Goddess or to ancient but by no means defunct or inaccessible Goddess traditions. To grasp this problem (the existence of which might be justifiably denied by many modern people identifying as pagans), we need to examine some of the popular notions concerning Goddess-nature. We shall concentrate particularly on the manifestation of these popular notions in the minds of men, but it must be remembered that any such difficult areas of emergence and changing awareness are shared by men and women, and are not by any means confined to physical gender.

One of the more obvious sources of confusion is in the popular familiarity with therapy, so rooted in our culture that many concepts have become "givens." Such givens tend to be bites from lengthy theories concerning the relationship between individual psychic archetypes and the feminine, the divine feminine, the ancient Great Goddess. Thus when a man identifies a sexual lover as mediating the Goddess, we could assume, or his therapist or counselor may assume, that this is due to some archetype of the feminine that our man has located upon the woman or man concerned.

It would seem that in many contemporary models of divine/human polarity the Goddess is expected to be either a lover or a mother; this limiting reductionism is found in varying degrees. If the Goddess is understood as merely a large reflected version of the conditioned images within our own psyche, rather than the true situation, in which we are reflections of her Universal Being, we have fallen back into the very trap from which Goddess-awareness is supposed to liberate us.

The regrettable result of the explanatory and reductionist effect is that men's notions of the Goddess herself are often limited to mere psychological stereotypes, both in terms of modern intellectual theory, and in the sense that this theory derives directly from religious propaganda. Such propaganda suppressed the true images and functions of the Goddess with the advent of monosexual patriarchal religion. Such hierarchical authoritarianism (refined but not invented by politicized Book Religions) was, and is, as damaging to men as to women, though it may take some bitter experience before men truly realize this and understand the full extent of the long-term damage done to them.

CHAPTER 3

Teachers and pupils

The personal teacher/mentor

Much emphasis has been placed upon the personal teacher mentor or guru in many contemporary and traditional systems of spiritual development. We can add to this the ubiquitous emphasis upon the therapist, a role that mimics the concept of the spiritual guide and teacher without necessarily fulfilling its original functions. Some, but by no means all, of this emphasis can clearly be traced back to the underlying concept of "the Masters," widely promoted by the Theosophical Society in the 19th century.[10]

Many modern ramifications depend strongly upon the cult of personality—the great teacher, leader, guru, savant, and so forth. In some cases the great one earns enormous sums of money, but more subtly he or (far less often) she, gains many more subtle benefits at the expense of pupils, patients, clients, or trainees.

What or who should the male seeking truth look for today? Does he need a direct personal guide or teacher as repeatedly emphasized in so many textbooks, courses or groups? Does the guru concept of the Eastern cultures work successfully for a Westerner? What does tradition, stripped of modern accretions or corruptions, tell us about the importance of a guide or teacher for inner development?

First, we should be aware that teachers or groups promoting systems of development, or therapy, or realization/revelation, for large sums of money are not, by their very nature, suitable for our needs. No inner development can be truly bought, only techniques and associated information: no true teacher can sell his or her deepest spiritual teaching. What, therefore, can we gain from a teacher at all?

The short answer to such questions is not enlightenment or empowerment, but skill. A teacher or mentor can help us develop very specific and easily recognizable skills, techniques, and disciplines. Often these skills are of a physical nature, an art, a craft, disciplines such as movement, coordination, and rigorous perception. There are complex and profound traditions of teaching physical skills that have underlying spiritual benefits: perhaps the best known of these today are the martial arts of the East, but there are many other examples found within arts, craft skills, dance, and theater.

The tuition of physical skills may indeed be justifiably charged as professional services: but anyone charging money for the benefit of our souls, our psychic or spiritual welfare, or for other subtle matters should be avoided. The saying attributed to Jesus of Nazareth in the New Testament still applies today, though its original political revolutionary significance (against Roman authority) is no longer pertinent: "Render unto Caesar that which is Caesar's, and unto God that which is God's." Today this wisdom applies to the charging of money by New Age gurus, therapies, channelers, and cult membership: if any such movements have a true spiritual quality, they need not demand money. There is a marketing ploy; if the spiritual teaching is really *secret*, really powerful, truly enlightening, then it has to be *expensive*. After all, anything of real value has a monetary equivalent, does it not? This tactic subtly leads to collecting a monied elite who think they are gaining something that is not made available to others. Strangely, this ploy often works.

Each level or world has its own energy and medium of exchange: material tokens cannot purchase subtle gifts or benefits. But subtle symbols or exchanges certainly can be made. Much of the tuition of the Mystery schools concerns such exchanges. If a good teacher can help us to acquire skills, which skills in turn help our inner development, we may, within reasonable limits, use such tuition as part of a spiritual or magical program of development, without seeking teachers who claim to sell us instant enlightenment. The skills, after all, are worthy of development in themselves, and any truthful teacher of inner development will tell you that only if you live through the various skills and arts wholly and utterly will they work upon deep levels. This is quite different from acquiring skills to inflate the ego, make money, or prove oneself.

A man seeking enlightenment or some level of change within the broad spectrum of the Male Mysteries today could indeed benefit from the skills that a good teacher has to offer, but skills do not of themselves comprise actual change or initiation. Any initiation sold for money is invalid, and may be weakening, as it has an implicit ulterior motive of profit. The profit can be more than monetary, for if we lose money to a fraudulent teacher, we learn a simple lesson in fiscal prudence. But if we lose autonomy, grace, or sovereignty, we can become soul-damaged, a more serious experience to recover from.

The traditional scenario of the pupil and teacher has often been misrepresented and misunderstood, but a brief analysis and restatement of the esoteric tradition which underpins such relationships in both East and West would be as follows:

The relationship between pupil and teacher in the inner Mysteries or magical and spiritual traditions is never limited to a one-to-one isolated situation. It always takes part within the broad and supportive framework of a tradition, Mystery, or school of development. Many such schools have long traditions and deep roots, manifesting in various forms in each century. While human mentors are often inspiring, much of the development within the Mysteries occurs in other realms of perception and transforming consciousness. Thus when a teacher and pupil work together they are within a holism, in an interrelated Mystery or structure of inner development.

There is a common misconception that the teacher–pupil relationship for men is like that of father and son: this is risky to assume, and has led to many emotional and spiritual problems. In modern therapy for men much emphasis seems to be placed upon loving and forgiving their fathers, transcending jealously, hatred, grief, pain, and so forth, particularly when those pains are focused upon the father from real or assumed childhood experiences. This process, unquestionably worthy and essential in contemporary society, plays little or no part in the Mysteries, and each male must eventually learn how to unfetter his love beyond self, beyond familial or relationship dynamics. Such loving-beyond -self includes parents, relatives, clan, race, and ultimately all that is.

The pupil–teacher relationship should not be limited to that of the kindly father and the developing reciprocating son. Some men pass themselves off as teachers or Masters to benefit from the emotional pain of their pupils, drawing upon and feeding on the energies of loss and love that have been imbalanced or frustrated in the pupil's childhood or teenage years. This tendency is sometimes found in certain therapists, New Age or commercial teachers and guides, psychic counselors, and cult leaders (regardless of the branch of religion that the cult derives from). We need hardly say that it is not confined solely to males, but is found across the range of such relationships.

There are a few little-known factors in the traditional teacher–pupil initiatory systems, which are worth disclosing and publishing, especially as they are often concealed by male initiates when they find pupils of their own.

The first, that of the span of tradition and its holism, is most important. The crude concept of a Master and pupil working solely together is simply untrue: most of the work is done upon inner imaginative levels, or in other dimensions of consciousness and energy. Such levels of consciousness and energy involve many other entities: mythic, transhuman, spiritual, ancestral, even down to the genetic or collective level. Thus the image of the older and younger male working in isolation and the wisdom being handed on as if it was a bundle of clothes or an especially tasty sandwich, is nonsense. Just as no man is an island, teacher and pupil never truly work together in intimate isolation.

Widely experienced, and least discussed, is the concept of initiatory role transfers in teacher/student relationships within the modern Mysteries. Terms such as this have come to be an accepted genre within psychotherapy, but the dynamics and deeper levels of this important reflection of energies have long been known within the esoteric traditions.

To simplify this theory and practice, we can express it in a typical example: A young man approaches a mature experienced teacher for initiation into the esoteric arts and disciplines (regardless of any specific tradition or religion, many of which could be fitted to this scenario). The teacher agrees, and begins training the pupil. But immediately a little-known factor begins to play a part: eventually, the Master and pupil roles will change, as the pupil will in turn become a Master. And so?

Is this not supposed to be the point of studying and initiation, to become an adept or teacher? Not at all; the aim of inner development is spiritual maturity and enlightenment; mastery is a coincidental occurrence, and must ultimately be disposed of. How do we dispose of it? By passing it onto a pupil, who will in turn pass it on to another pupil, and so on.

So many men are desperate to acquire the Mantle of their spiritual or magical teacher, but only the initiate truly knows what this Mantle is, for it has a potential negative process within it. Yet only *potentially* negative, depending utterly on how it is handled.

The Mantle comes from the accumulated soul-burden or karma of a long line of initiates, which is realigned with every wearer, and passed on to the willing pupil. The teacher is left free of this Mantle at death, or in rarer cases, during a lifetime. The pupil takes it willingly, knowing that the burden will eventually pass from him to another. Originally this was a valid and beneficent system: in early cultures it worked well, for each initiate took on a burden of responsibility from within the Order or Mystery, and carried it and attempted to resolve it through work in the inner and outer worlds. This acceptance includes certain tasks that are truly long term, working toward the transformation of human consciousness. It also includes taking your Master's mistakes and their longer-term implications.

Initiatory techniques still found in esoteric or magical development today can, and often do, pass on such karmic burdens to unwitting pupils. Unscrupulous adepts who have learned this method will repeatedly try to pass their karmic burden to younger pupils, but usually fail to do so. This is one of the typical loose ends and problems of male initiation in the modern era, a hangover from earlier times that has never been properly erased, discussed, or balanced.

The problem of the Mantle does not, interestingly, apply to women, who inherit or gain a different kind of responsibility at initiation. Once again, the difference is defined by the physical entity, the gender, and not by inner qualities, sexual preference, skills or levels of development. Polarity is everything that endures in the work of the Mysteries, while personality is infinitely malleable and ephemeral.

Working with inner-world teachers

One of the proven methods of inner or transpersonal development, is through working with metaphysical teachers. The word metaphysical is used quite deliberately here, in its proper sense: in the Male Mysteries (as in all historic Mysteries) it is possible, even essential, to learn from and work with transhuman entities that are not physical, but nevertheless have vibrant existence in other states or dimensions of consciousness and energy. In this chapter we shall consider briefly what such states, dimensions and entities truly are.

The technique is an ancient sacromagical one, found in all perennial wisdom traditions and (attenuated) in religions worldwide. When we apply it specifically to male development, however, certain clear parameters begin to appear, and certain specific inner-world teachers, adepts, and mythic or divine entities can be emphasized. While many of these entities are masculine, some of the major figures are feminine. This is such an important matter that it needs to be repeatedly affirmed: some of the major transforming and enabling entities found in the initiations of the Male Mysteries are feminine. without these figures, archetypes, entities, or goddesses (call them what we will) no man can possibly develop: just as he could not have been conceived and brought to birth without a physical mother. Yet we should not assume for one moment that all such feminine figures in the Male Mysteries are motherly; many are quite unmotherly and a few can be terrifying.

For the present, however, let us set aside the higher mythic figures of gods and goddesses, and concentrate on the teachers, adepts or Masters that are commonly found in meditative and visualizing work. These tend, for many men, to be male, just as for many women, the inner-world teachers tend to be female. There are no firm rules to such matters, and much depends upon the individual and the techniques employed. One of the most powerful teaching traditions available to a male, for example, involves learning from an inner-world order of priestesses: this is a quite specific and recognizable Branch of the Mysteries, often though not exclusively connected to the tradition and Mystery of the Sacred Kingship (Chapter 7).

We should be cautious when assessing techniques that we wish to learn and practice. Many of the pitfalls and delusions concerning so-called Masters are discussed shortly, and the line between beneficial inner work and absurdity, between inspiration and dangerous delusion, is sometimes rather thin.

For the present we can set aside specialized contact, such as that of the sisterhood described above, and consider the general technique of contacting and working with inner-world teachers, usually, but not exclusively, appearing as male figures for male students. But what do we mean by "appearing as male figures"?

We can dispose of the comic-book nonsense concerning super-males who appear physically to humble groveling students in order to inculcate better forms of humanity. At best this level of understanding provides a potential threshold into the true initiatory techniques and other dimensions, hopefully one which is crossed and then recognized for the delusion that it is. At worst this type of fantasy leads to racism, and what could be termed evil or black magic. The concept of a male superhuman elite should play no part in true spiritual development.

So how do the teachers appear? The answer is through a technique of bridge-building or form-energizing. First, we must decide what kind of teacher we think we need, and this in itself is no easy task. Next, we should find an image or description of such a teacher: traditionally such images are found in ancient poems, texts, myths, or legends, long enshrined in human consciousness, and frequently tend to relate to semi-historical characters. The range of magicians, wise men, warriors, poets, and kings is wide and deep. This protean rambling and often vague traditional range is, paradoxically, the safest and most precise to work with. We shall return to it shortly.

Other contacts are those specific inner-world adepts or teachers that play a role in magical or spiritual orders and groups, often spanning long periods of time. These tend to be more historically defined personae; there is an advanced technique through which it is possible to tune in to the persona of almost any historical man or woman for inner-world contact, education, and interaction. This level of working is easily confused, and requires considerable practice; we shall set it aside for the present, merely stating that it is not spiritualism, or working with those who are deceased. Perhaps the nearest equivalent to this technique is that of ancestral contact found in the primal religions and ethnic magical arts, or that of the ancestral and hero contacts developed in the Classical cultures of the ancient world.

Identifying inner-world teachers

There is a tendency for popular and literary images of inner-world teachers to be pure, holy, and very unreal. This is an enervating concept, and, contrary to what might be believed, is relatively modern. The ancient gods and goddesses, for example, were never stereotypes or idealized images. They did indeed represent certain specific powers, but always had attached to them or present within them other facets of energy, nature, and even eccentricities of divine personality. Modern psychology has taken up myth, particularly that of the Greeks, and employed it as a model giving insights into the human psyche and personality. This is fine, but it only goes a small way toward a true understanding of the gods and goddesses and their potential within human spiritual development.

When we come to inner-world teachers, the picture is more complex. Modern images of pure shining Masters are usually part of some business plan or manipulative scenario. Ancestral myths, legends, and folk tales can reveal the true nature of the wise man or woman, and inner-world teachers will appear in many guises. A general rule might be as follows:

If your inner-world teacher appears to you in meditation or vision as a pure shining superhuman, he or she is almost certainly a fantasy or even a fake. Certain teachers may appear in a frivolous role, but will always offer some deeper sense of identity and purpose to the meditator, which has to be picked up, attuned to, and opened out. After this exchange or period of proving and clarification, the nonsensical aspect of the inner-world contact vanishes, leaving a clearer identity. Teaching may often be given in the form of a game or jest, and may occur during the most superficial first contacts, so we need not assume that all inner-world teaching is a solemn or ponderous affair. Indeed, the best teachers always have a deep sense of humor, which is the hallmark of true spiritual development and awareness.

In practice we may encounter inner-world teachers as a result of meditations and visualizations. The contact may be unseen or as far as we are concerned, unconscious; it may be fully conscious, or of varying degrees of mutual awareness in between. Some teaching entities make themselves known to the meditating consciousness only by signs or symbols. These tend to be either non-human beings, or inner-world sources that are working in a higher octave of consciousness than our own. In some cases, the higher octaves of consciousness will manifest through an inner-world persona, but there is no requirement that this persona or mask be a genuine historical person, even if it presents itself as such. As with the traditions of gods and goddesses, no time and space will be wasted herein by trying to prove the existence of inner-world teachers; if we use the methods of the Mystery, we will discover the truth for ourselves.

The simplest and most effective method of working is well established in tradition, and needs only a little adaptation for modern use. Originally, inner-world characters were defined through sets of oral tales, poems, ballads, and ritual drama. Such personae were also used in the more advanced stages of imagination, envisioning, and meditation. We all know, for example, of the power of the image of Merlin, a figure from Celtic tradition. He remains powerful even today, despite the accumulated nonsense which overlays the original persona or entity in enduring popular imagination and entertainment.[11]

In contemporary use we can define certain types of personae, types of image. These are built up in visualization, and eventually take on a life of their own. That is all that there is to it. The imagination attunes to an image, such as those defined in our exercises in later chapters, and eventually a true inner contact enlivens that image or construct. This is the method that was used in ancient temple practices; an icon image/statue was imbued, through telesmic magic, creating a clear connection to its deity. No one worshipped a symbolic statue, but felt the presence, the telesm of the divine, attuned to the physical image. The presentation of carved or iconic images persists to this day in many variants of Christianity, though this is often considered to be idolatry by other branches of the Book Religions.

When the contact occurs, the image will often change. Sometimes the true inner-world teacher appears from behind or within, or to one side of the image, and we can eventually dispose of our starting image altogether. Sometimes the image itself intensifies and comes more alive; the entire matter is one for careful judgment and common sense, set into balance with imaginative and intuitive work. Not an easy task, you might say, yet we all have an inherent pattern ability or system of imagination and awareness that enables us to perform most of these functions quite naturally. We must release the grid, the conditioning of our modern culture; not too much at first, but just enough to explore new dimensions of freedom without dysfunction.

The degree of energy and ability, however, varies from person to person. It is only if we try to force our inherent abilities (in what is assumed to be an act of willpower or some other pseudo-manly notion) that we either get no result, or some type of inflated fantasy. Many typical male inner or spiritual problems arise from the concepts of manliness, willpower, and so forth. Sometimes these enervating notions are disguised in the form of purity or transcendent aims; but they are, nevertheless, just muscle-flexing. The image or Branch of the Warrior is kept in balance by concepts of honor and service. His strength, skill, and discipline is nothing in itself, but everything in service to a spiritual reality greater than the individual. The man who ignores this truth becomes a bully, an oppressor and eventually destroys himself through isolation from loving interaction, from reality. Sadly he often takes others with him on the way to destruction.

The Masters, but not hidden

A relatively large proportion of the spiritual and magical literature of our contemporary world, ranging from the sources of orthodox religions in both East and West to very recent New Age publications, deals with the wide (though not always deep) subject of the Masters. In formal religion they were often defined as saints or demigods; in Western esoteric or sacromagical and New Age literature, the concept of successful intercession between saints and higher forms of divinity has gradually been reduced, but the concept of superhuman or transhuman Masters has been greatly developed. The entire subject is fraught with problems, and suffers greatly from the power politics of male-dominated spirituality. Many men come to the inner arts or traditions of transpersonal development seeking to become Masters; few attain to, or retain, this initial desire. We might first consider if the Masters actually exist, and, if they do, what role they play in human life, and what relationship they have to the development of other men along inner transpersonal or spiritual paths. First, we should dispose of some of the more pernicious fantasy regarding Masters that has appeared in the last 150 years.

This is best assessed by briefly examining the difference between earlier concepts of transhuman or highly developed beings, and the relatively modern concepts of inner-world or spiritual or magical Masters and adepts. As a popular T-shirt states: "If there are Hidden Masters, what are they hiding from?"

When we examine the wide range of literature and tradition available to us on the subject, we find a progressive change occurring, which has greatly accelerated from the 19th century onward, though there are clear indications of it in earlier sources. Recent concepts of the Masters or adepts seem to revolve around superhuman males, usually with an insistence upon physical immortality or immense longevity. These males are said to have special powers, are supposed to oversee the reputed evolution of the human race. With each war, each ruthless act of massive exploitation of nature and of fellow humans, we may think that the Masters are substantially more inept than adept. They supposedly live in remote mountainous regions such as the Andes or the Himalayas, and are said to make both physical and non-physical communications only to chosen pupils or channelers. Because the pupils are special, or chosen, the rest of us have to deal with the Masters through the favored pupils. Does the model seem familiar? It is merely another version of the religious model, whereby only a professional priesthood (male) has access to the jealous god (male) who lives upstairs.

Various cults and movements have sprung up around the central concept of a group of Masters. The best known of these is the 19th-century Theosophical Society, which has had a far-reaching effect upon subsequent societies, orders, cults, and upon much New Age literature and related practices. The basic pattern is simple and has been often repeated; someone declares that he or she is in contact with an individual Master or group of Hidden Masters or adepts: the contacted beings communicate teachings and direct instructions, and encourage the forming of a cult, group, or society. The group develops, disseminates literature and various initiatory techniques; people use the teachings to develop themselves, or for specific aims within the structure of human society. Usually, the boundaries between such intentions are (perhaps intentionally) blurred, and there is a constant shifting of membership as people reassess their own aims and values (at best) or simply become bored with the current fashion that such a group or society represents.

There can be no doubt that unscrupulous operators can set themselves up to become rich by this simple system; there is also little doubt that there are many people involved in such groups that genuinely work with sincerity, and truly believe in the structure that they uphold. The reality of the Masters, however, is a quite different question to the veracity or honesty of their followers. In some ways, it does not matter if the reputed Masters are entirely false, for the boundary between a real entity and an imaginative construct is forever shifting; this applies to ourselves as humans just as much as it does to other forms of entity.

We might tend initially to dispose of the whole subject as immature nonsense, particularly when we consider the range of Masters who seem to be readily available to various groups and sects. If we combine these with the large number of saints and demigods and heroes in world religions, we might be justified in asking why these hundreds of superhuman beings have not gained substantially more for the humanity they are supposed to oversee. There is often a trite answer to this burning question, which is: "you are not ready yet." We might be inclined to respond with the famous quote from Rabbi Hillel: "If not now, when?"[12] But let us leave such shameless cynicism aside, and look more deeply at the esoteric or hidden aspects of the subject.

First, there can be little doubt that the prevalence of male Masters or adepts (be they fantasy or fact) is due to the political religious situation of male supremacy. It is significant upon a number of levels that modern mediums or channelers are frequently women, who mediate male teachers or Masters. We seldom come across a male channeler who mediates a female Master, or should it be a Hidden Mistress? So ingrained is the concept of male mastery or adepthood that it passes unquestioned in many cases. Unquestioned even by wise intelligent people who enter into transpersonal or spiritual disciplines.

If we are generous, and admit that there may be more to such mediumship than stereotypes of male-dominated pseudo-wisdom, then we might see in modern practices the remnants of earlier systems of mediumship deriving from the temple practices of the ancient world. We know that in ancient cultures women often acted as channels for male powers such as gods, heroes, or spirits. We have, however, lost the inverse, well established in the past, that men may mediate female energies and entities.

The ingrained concept of the all-male Master is a serious hindrance to male development, and until it is totally removed from the individual man's consciousness he probably will not make any true or lasting progress upon the inner paths. Once again we touch upon the important subject of balanced polarity: an all-male adepthood or priesthood, or an individual male who assumes that he has an inalienable right to superiority is essentially a weak unbalanced form. Ultimately a bitter price is paid for such one-sided monosexual development within priesthood, adepthood, mastery; and all too often, it is we, the supposed inferiors, that are required to pay. Money is the least valuable form of payment, for we pay in subtle ways with our hopes and dreams.

In Eastern religions, there are many female saints or inner-world mentors, but they are less prevalent in the West. In any case, these transhuman beings tend to blur with mythic non-human figures.

Even historical saints or Masters seem to fuse with mythic beings, gods, or in the case of female saints, goddesses. Somewhere along the line of historical movement, the emphasis has been stripped from the mythic and placed upon the fantastic or superhuman. In contemporary entertainment, fantasy and simulation is stacked and strained until the imagination is overloaded and exhausted by superpowers, bulging muscles, despicable villainy and ever-growing technical wonders (especially explosions and cataclysms). This ongoing rapid change toward extreme fantasy is, paradoxically, related to the development of scientific materialism. Without the technology (developed for profit), we would not have the means of replacing our inherent inner imagination with an external exteriorized fantasy dependent upon a glass screen and microchips.

While the much popularized New Age Hidden Masters are supposed to be spiritual entities, they tend to be removed from the mainstream of human myth and religion. We can detect several strands woven and colored with this changing pigmentation: the most obvious of these are lust for power, longing for immortality. Such desires are projected upon idealized images of super-males. Such desires may, initially, be harnessed as strong motivation for discipline, learning, gaining skill, but they are ultimately barriers to true transpersonal realization.

The situation is a typical initiatory paradox; a man longs for power, longevity, even immortality, but by working through the disciplines that are supposed to lead to such gains, he loses his obsessive quest and desire, and it is replaced by a new horizon of consciousness. For a few fortunate men, this change is gradual. But for the majority of males it may come as a series of drastic initiatory experiences, intense catabolic or breaking and destroying forces resonating through not only inner perception, but the entire life pattern, permeating outer structures such as relationships, family, friends, and work. The very things that he has hoped to gain by becoming a Master such as security, freedom, superiority, are all dashed away.

After such painful initiations, we may begin upon the path to true mastery, which is nothing like the popular idea so widely promulgated.

CHAPTER 4

Polarity and sexuality

Polarity

Let us consider some of the basics of polarity, working within the Male Mysteries. As we are intentionally working within a masculine situation, vital feminine counterparts are defined as inner-world visions, entities, and goddesses. This way of working reveals both our weaknesses and strengths. It must ultimately lead, however, to both sexes working together physically, mentally, emotionally, and spiritually. Many men and women are not ready or able to undertake such work, no matter how willing. The initiations of the Male Mysteries prepare us and mature us for further spiritual life, by which we must mean all levels of life through into physical expression, in the broadest human consciousness.

Men can damage themselves by seeking to correct problems in their lives through joining groups, undertaking therapies of various sorts, and falling into the trap that money can buy spirit. In recent years an elite method called "mindfulness" has been aimed at professionals in the technology industries, where there is intense stress and pressure to constantly deliver results. Drawn from enduring Eastern precepts, mindfulness has been criticized for offering a purportedly therapeutic technique without the corresponding spiritual teachings that are found within Buddhism.[13]

This type of theme, of technique without inner spirit or deep spiritual attainment and commitment, is especially appealing to men. Another frequent problem for men is that they will sometimes confuse inner forces and simple sexuality. Women seem less prone to the subtle levels of this confusion.

Many people with a genuine (or superficial) interest in spiritual or magical matters, who simply desire one another, like to believe that there is some great magically portentous situation at work. Rather than simply indulge in healthy sexual activity, they can concoct absurd and potentially unhealthy magical or spiritual scenarios and situations for themselves. The favorite one is:

Past Lives

One way of cleaning up confusion over Past Lives is to meditate upon a simple truth, self-evident: all Lives are Present Lives. Are you reading this page and thinking that as you do so you are in a past life? Wherever a life may seem to be in terms of the fragmented lens of history, we are always and only in the Present. Thus many Past Lives are simultaneous; past and future lives are at one, all are in the present. Yet we have a filtering mechanism, that restricts our perceptions and memories; it is constantly at work in our current and still present life. Imagine how maddening and burdensome it would be to remember every little detail of your life thus far, then think about remembering every past life. Our healthy filters of consciousness have been developed over many thousands of years; if we wish to move beyond them, we must be ready to rebuild with something better. The Mysteries help us with this task.

People spend much time agonizing over Past Lives, and assuming that they are drawn to one another as the result of something in such Past Lives, rather than the fact there is a simple sexual current between them. Unscrupulous people (often, but not always, men) may manipulate past-life scenarios to seduce victims.

Sexual initiation

In ancient cultures the much-misunderstood art of temple sexuality (often disparagingly called temple prostitution) was used to bring men and women into a full realization of their own energies, emotions, and spiritual potential. It is rare indeed today for a man to experience this type of initiation from a woman, and probably rarer still for a woman to experience it from a man, but not entirely unknown or impossible. Same-sex couples have the same dynamic situation; profound sexual initiation is rare for us all.

Sexual initiation is a term used freely by anthropologists, psychologists, and social workers, with no concept of its deeper meaning or potential. What they are referring to is not true spiritual initiation through sexual exchange, but initial sexual experiences that can mold a man's energy pattern for much of his lifetime. Certainly, true sexual initiations should also be the initial sexual experiences of any life cycle, but this seldom occurs today.

We might loosely define a typical sequence of development as follows: the male student begins transformation by developing, through traditional training and visionary exercises. At a somewhat later stage he might work with other men, including but not limited to interaction with, and tuition from, a more experienced teacher. There is a shocking lack of such group situations for male spiritual and magical development, for we cannot truthfully count orthodox religion as being deeply concerned with spiritual empowerment and liberation.

Nothing in the case history of orthodox religion gives us evidence to show that it is committed to human liberty or inner transformation. For such means of development, we have to seek outside formal religion, in the so-called heretical and suppressed cults, in the esoteric and native magical traditions. Clearly, this search is fraught with problems and dangers, and of course orthodox propaganda tells us that no man or woman should seek inner development, but that we should remain content to be obedient and merely worship within a controlled system of soul trading.

However, there is a true case to be made for occasionally remaining within a defined religious framework. If you have deep belief and your intuition tells you that a particular Church or religion will continue to meet your spiritual needs, no one can nay-say this, and you should remain within such a structure. If you participate in a religious framework, the liberation comes from within yourself, drawn out by the very restrictions of dogma and faith. The ways to empowerment and psychic liberation are many, and the esoteric traditions of affiliation are not for the faint-hearted or weak-willed. Indeed, the orthodox propaganda is truer today than ever, for it could be applied to the plethora of money-seeking cults, orders, groups, techniques, channelers, healers, advisers, gurus, teaching systems, processes, and the like that feed off our gullibility, our loneliness, our weakness, our desperate need to find direction in a meaningless and dying world. At least a religion may hold some vestiges of an ancient spiritual foundation within it, albeit deeply buried.

Homosexuality

(There is an increasing tendency to use the word homosexual to apply only to male/male sexual preference. It has always meant same-sex sexuality, regardless of male or female.)

Here we are going to touch upon a very sensitive and hotly debated set of interlaced ideas, revelations, activities, and fervent beliefs. Once again, there is no intention herein to prove anything, only to explore the dynamics of polarity that may affect our celebration of, and participation within, the Male Mysteries.

One of the rapidly transforming features of the ferment of the 20th and 21st centuries has been an increasing openness and declaration of homosexuality. "Coming out," asserting, accepting, respecting. The feminist pagan movement has frequently associated Goddess worship and the revival of feminine power with lesbian sexual preference. Many gay men and women associate themselves strongly with the cause of freedom and equality for people of homosexual preference, male or female. We are not attempting here to offer a social or political study of such declarations and associated movements, but to explore some of their inner aspects, particularly where they relate to the Male Mysteries.

There are two issues that seem to have become confused, which can cause unnecessary suffering and difficulty in terms of spiritual development.

The first issue is that of the simple right of any person, male or female or other, to express and live his, her, or their sexual preference; some great strides have been made along this path for the LGBTQ communities, but there is still much work to be done.

The second issue is that of the overall relationship of men and women, regardless of sexual orientation or preference: as lovers, as friends, as brothers and sisters.

Many feminists practicing Goddess worship deny or reject the possibility of relationships with men, and embrace lesbianism, sometimes suggesting that it is particularly blessed by the Goddess. We hear fewer assertions made by modern men concerning worship of the God, yet we do find a hidden shadow of male homosexuality running deeply through traditional Christianity, and in Christian writings and monastic practices. This is not unhealthy because it is homosexuality, but only because it is hidden under the cloak of moralizing anti-feminism, and so becomes part of the long-running deep campaign for suppression and denial of anything feminine in humanity.

Men suffer from suppression of the feminine, just as women do, though the male damage is often hidden under an illusion of supremacy, false superiority, and entitlement. This illusion of supremacy is reinforced in each generation but is essentially founded upon fear and the imbalance of energies. Men have not been allowed to truly touch women, or for that matter other men, for centuries. No wonder we have such problems in our society. Once the Goddess was officially removed from recognition in human life, the entire cycle of energies became imbalanced and consequently spun into an unnatural pattern.

One certain thing we do know; people tend to relate sexually to one another; this is simply a matter of polarity, with male and female entities, or positive and negative, polarities exchanging sexual energies in various ways. Universal Being tends toward polarized, and cyclic and therefore temporary patterns of energy. In the case of humanity these manifest as body gender, and operate as sexual attraction.

While there is nothing in the Mysteries or in esoteric tradition that condemns male or female homosexuality, there is an immense amount of information on polarity and the use of polarized energies in magical and spiritual development. The techniques of inner development often rely strongly upon sexually polarized imagery. More simply, we are taught that if we use our imagination powerfully, working with specific sets of images, we will experience transformation. The esoteric traditions uphold special techniques and images which give known results, and which have persisted, often underground, for many centuries.

While any one of us has a simple right to exercise his or her sexual preference without persecution, no one has the right to insist that the Goddess especially blesses lesbians and that men are redundant. Nor is there any right to male political and religious supremacy or a covert male homosexuality, in a religious context, that suppresses women. We must be constantly made aware of our deep-rooted and complex confusions between sexual preference and sexual magic, or between sexual roles in society and sexually defined religious belief.

In our present context of the Male Mysteries, we should consider the question of homosexuality as it relates to the techniques which we have suggested for inner development. There is still a pejorative unfortunate tendency to think that queer/gay men are somehow cut off from magical or spiritual development because of their sexual preference: this is not so. This type of opinion has been voiced publicly by various revivalist pagans and magicians, who assume, quite wrongly, that the ancient gods and goddesses are only concerned with heterosexual sexuality as an aspect of fertility and the cycles of nature in breeding and fecundity. The inference is that homosexuality is against the fertility magic of the Old Ones. This is exactly the type of dangerous nonsense running deeply through orthodox political religion in the West, where homosexuality was loudly condemned yet secretly practiced. There are, furthermore, many subtle ramifications to such concepts, which may appear to be trivial in many ways, yet have a devastatingly powerful effect. When we see such concepts emerging in the revival of paganism witchcraft or magic, they are almost undoubtedly immature hangovers from a materialist post-Christian upbringing and cultural ambience. By way of balancing such situations, the pagan, witchcraft, and magical communities have strong continents of LGBTQ members, and many recognize the Sacred Other as being essential to human evolution of consciousness and energy.

The ancestral pagan world seems to have made little difference between homosexuality and heterosexuality; it was all sexuality, and all blessed by the powers of the Mother and Father, no matter by what names the divinities were called.[14] We can see, however, some aspects of Classical Greek culture, the beginning of that Hellenist intellectual trend toward male exclusivism, which was eventually taken up by developing Christianity, and warped into the most damaging set of indoctrinations and cruelties that has ever passed itself off as a religion of love.

A short summary of this ever-open discussion is that each individual is uniquely different from any other, and that mature relationships are not based upon stereotypical self-indulgent sex, but upon a wide variety of interwoven factors in which physical sexual activity and gender preference play a moderate but significant part.

There is no need for men reviving the Male Mysteries to take a step backward into the ignorance and prejudice that has dominated the Western world for more than 2,000 years. Indeed, most of the arts and practices of the esoteric traditions derive from pre- or non-Christian sources (without ever denying or rejecting the core of a possibly true spiritual Christianity), and if we use them correctly, we can bypass the terrible inheritance of monosexual oppressive religion.

Basic human rights have, in the 20th century, become intertwined with deeper realities of polarity and sexuality. This is hardly surprising, as it is only recently that we have been able to talk openly with one another, male or female, and assert sexual rights at all. Is it just possible that the men of the 21st century may be able to gain a balanced understanding of this problem? Men will find new ways as they emerge from a long period of monosexual religion, deliberately designed to suspend men in a frozen state of vicious immaturity, open to manipulation and thus willing to manipulate others in turn. Men are, or should soon be, ready to take a huge leap forward.

We might be inclined to think that the use of god- and goddess-forms, certain male and female archetypes, and the associated techniques described in this book need to be somehow reversed for gay men to use successfully. This is not so, for the archetypes and god-forms both transcend and underpin human sexuality, male and female, hetero- and homosexual. It is often the case that upon inner levels the current sexual preference (be it heterosexual, homosexual, or bisexual) becomes irrelevant. There is always a threshold beyond which our sexual energy becomes aroused in a higher octave, and does not necessarily require physical gratification. This should not, incidentally, become confused with devious propaganda concerning spirituality and the rejection of the body. In the Mysteries, the body is always sacred whatever its sexual attunement, for it is the vehicle of the God and Goddess conjoined, who are themselves vehicles of the Universal Being.

The open secret for gay/queer or bisexual men and women in the esoteric tradition is to try not to intellectually alter the images such as god- and goddess-forms or archetypes and personae, but to use them to gain insight into one's own strengths and weaknesses. The archetypes and divine forms are surprisingly consistent through the centuries, and only change slowly and organically within the collective consciousness. Furthermore, they are preserved by intentional magical work and concentrated vision as telesms. This is the difference between a powerful finely tuned archetype, telesm, or magical image, and the generalized archetypes defined by psychology.

A typical example of manipulation of images is the removal of the Goddess from official worship, other than in her attenuated form as Virgin. More subtle examples are found in the imagery of Tarot decks, developed from certain key pagan images in poetry, storytelling and iconography. These images were progressively adapted into cards by the 16th century, and modified to fit suppressive propagandist images representing both Church and State.[15] Examples include: The Devil (Horned God), The Pope (Hierophant of the Mysteries), The Emperor (Compassionate Ruling deity), Death as a skeleton, using imagery from the Black Death pandemic (but originally the pagan Dark Goddess of death and change), Judgment as the Christian apocalypse, but originally a cosmic image of the Weaver Goddess, such as *Ananke* in Plato's Republic.[16]

At a later stage of our inner work, we may, if necessary, reposition images and archetypes upon the Wheel of Life. As a rule the placement of god-forms and archetypes for meditation and visualization remains inflexible in early training, and only when the individual has a good understanding of, and ability with, the forms and the imaging techniques may we start moving them around the Sacred Directions, within ourselves, and in dedicated spaces such as a meditation room or temple. This conscious location of images and concepts also relates to the esoteric aspects of the Art of Memory.[17]

For most of us this Great Work is done inwardly, and in a simple sense male and female variations of sexual preference might be said to arise from a variant placing of the archetypes within the energy field of the Directions. The causes of such variable appropriate location of power images cannot be expressed so easily; it may be represented astrologically in a natal chart, or it may be accessed through deep intuition into what sometimes appear to be Past Lives, but such methods, and there are many of them, merely offer us a rationalization of inner truths. The key is always to work with the inner truth rather than try to excessively label it or explain it. Most important of all, we should never use ready-made, one size fits all, systems that forcibly relate our inner truths to conformist doctrines: that is the way of slavery and destruction. When we come to the practical work described in the later chapters, it is flexible, and eventually each man builds his own version, functioning alone or within a group.

It is through mediation (as distinct from meditation) and magic, that our inner energies are located as entities, and we work with the truth of their relationships, upon the Wheel of Life. This long-enduring method has not been adequately reassessed for modern use, and holds a vast store of knowledge and understanding, which we have yet to unravel and render fitting for future development.

We must make a firm distinction here between mature sexual and emotional clarity, potentially within us all, regardless of our sexual preference or attractions, and an average male–female sexual polarization. That which has long been regarded as "normal," can often be replete with viciousness, perversion, cruelty, and delusion. It is the qualities of the individual that are important, and how they live and behave with regard to others, not the mere fact of sexual preference.

There is nothing in the Male Mysteries that bars the LGBTQ person from development, but there is still much within ourselves, heterosexual, homosexual, bisexual, non-binary, or other, that may do so.

The ancients made little distinction between the sexual encounters of men and women, men and men, women and women. It was all sexuality, part of the flow of energies in nature between different beings. This important concept, however, should not be confused or intentionally warped into a license for manipulative sexual behavior. Too often, revival paganism and magic has been little more than a vehicle for the sexual preferences of group leaders and their members. Nothing could be further from the ancient paradigm in which sexuality was only one beautiful part of a unified view of nature, of people, and of relationship to the land, the planet, and the stars.

There are many possible reasons why Christianity in particular has attempted such extreme suppression of homosexuality and bisexuality, while maintaining a distinctly unhealthy corrupting undercurrent of sexual entitlement and homosexuality for men only, within its political and psychological structure. Recent and ongoing revelations of sexual abuse by the priesthood of the Roman Catholic Church show how cloudy undercurrents swirling around the hollow rocks of celibacy and autocratic authority can lead to intentional wickedness and absence of compassion.

From an esoteric perspective, the rejection of physical love and sexual activity between members of the same sex, especially between males, is perhaps connected to the collection or possession of souls. To elaborate, male homosexuality and its suppression goes hand in hand with the concept of the rigid sanctified marriage, female subservience, male dominance, and the demand that women submit to breeding without any option of contraception. The general theme seems to be that souls must be generated and conditioned within one religion only, eventually overtaking all others by the sheer weight of numbers.

Historically we find that free sexual expression was often an integral part of the worship of the Great Goddess. Many of the rites and techniques of the ancient temples involved sexuality, though perhaps not as in any lurid entertainment fantasy of such techniques. One of the major aims of developing political Christianity was to remove the souls of humanity from such Goddess religion and such sexual initiatory rites, the better to control them.

Homosexual males, which is to say physical males with inner polarities that may be predominantly male or female but tend to relate physically to other men, were said to be especially blessed by the Goddess. At the risk of generating hostility among Goddess feminists, including some of my own friends, I would propose that lesbians might well have been especially blessed by the God. This aspect of magical or spiritual polarity seems to have been lost or suppressed. And yet, just as the monk focuses intensely upon the Virgin and St Sebastian, so does the nun focus upon Jesus and St Theresa.

In Part II, we will explore the Five Branches of the Male Mysteries, leading to our practical work in Part III.

PART II

WARRIOR, POET, PROPHET, PRIEST, KING

CHAPTER 5

Warrior, Poet, Prophet, Priest, King

We may summarize the transformative Branches or modes of the Male Mysteries as follows: Warrior, Poet, Prophet, Priest, King.

These Five Branches focus upon the King as a central or pivotal image, while the Worker or Man is the source and sum of them all. Figure 5 shows the relationships between the Branches. Each Branch has a traditional correspondence to the human body, as shown in Figure 6. These correspondences are of immense value in meditation, and show the subtle interplay of male energies.

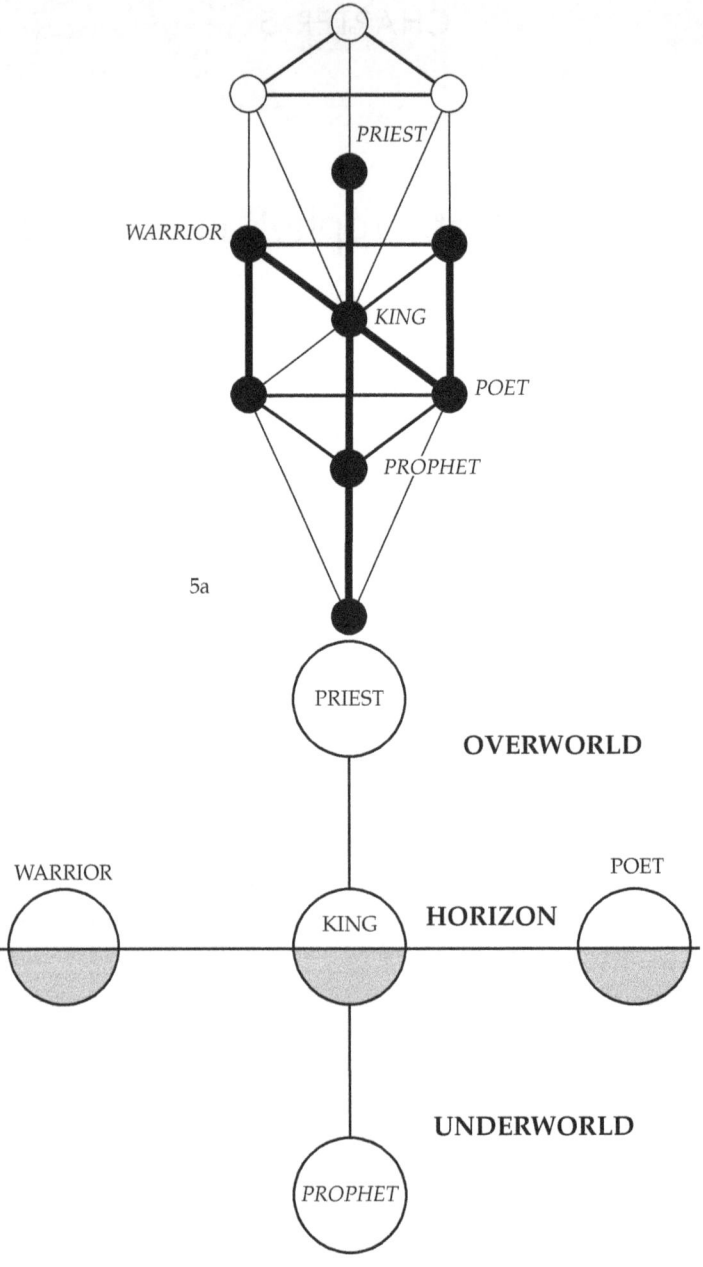

Figure 5: The Five Branches.

The Five Branches of the Male Mysteries are: Warrior, Poet, Priest, Prophet, King. The Four Companions of Warrior, Poet, Priest, and Prophet are embodiments of energy in male form, and each has both a goddess- and a god-within or behind them at deeper levels (see Chapter 10). The King and/or Worker is the primal man, both in his simplest, unrealized state, and in full awareness and balance through the transformations and enabling effects of work with the other branches, companions, gods and goddesses.

The Five Branches are located upon the Wheel of Life (see Figure 1), and are broadly associated with the Directions and Elements. These associations are not dogmatic or rigid, and may vary from person to person and time to time, but tend to appear in polarized patterns as shown. They may also be located upon the Tree of Life (see Figure 2) which shows the mythic, mental, emotional, and physical harmonic connections.

A further pattern that repays meditation is that of the Horizon or sacred land (planetary surface) and the Underworld and Overworld. The wounded or incomplete King is healed and transformed through the regenerative power of the Underworld, held in balance between Priest above and Prophet below, and the cyclic forces of Poet and Warrior upon the Horizon, to right and left. This holism is shown again in connection to the human body in Figure 6.

Five is the number of man, by which we should mean not something dominantly male, but male, female and bisexual beings with five digits, able to perform variable manual activities (Man and manual come from the root word manus or hand, with derivatives such as manufacture, manage, manipulate, and manuscript. These are not derived from man as male, but from the Latin word for hand). Unfortunately, the word mankind is seen today as an inclusive male term for humanity, when in fact it means "handed beings."

The four fingers and thumb enable the skills of humanity, through manipulation in the true sense of the word with no negative implications ... a musician manipulates his or her instrument, an artist manipulates the brush, a computer programmer the keyboard. Such skills work through polarity or harmonious opposition between thumb and fingers. All mental activity manipulates the stuff of consciousness, thought, emotion, and imagination by our inner equivalent of the hand, the Five Branches of the will, working through polarity. The thumb represents the King and Worker, while the four fingers represent the Four Companions.

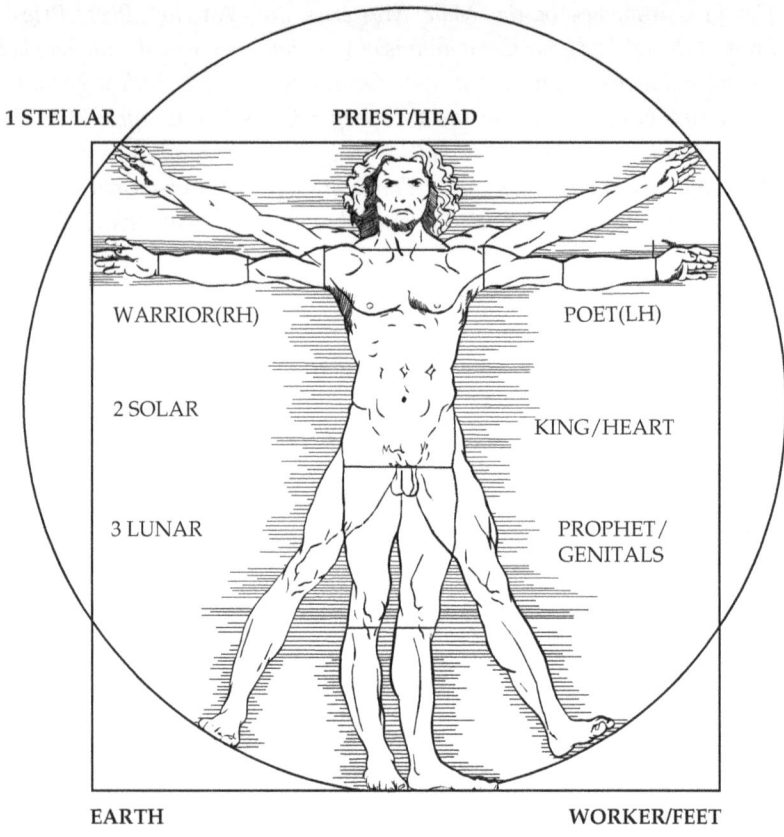

Figure 6: The Five Branches and the male body.

Traditional attributes of the Five Branches and the human body are reiterated in modern theories of right and left brain functions. Both the traditional and modern models of man are indications of a deeper pattern of polarized energy within humanity, mirroring patterns of Universal Being.

1. Head/Priest/Stellar Direction (above)/Spirit or transpersonal being/ Third Threshold.
2. Left Hand side (right brain)/Poet/Compassion.
3. Right Hand side (left brain)/Warrior/Severity.
4. Heart/King/Solar Direction (center)/soul and mind/Second Threshold.

5. Genitals/Prophet/Lunar Direction (below center)/sexuality and habitually unconscious mind/Underworld/First Threshold.
6. Feet/Man of Earth/Sacred Land or planet/outer or manifest form and body.

The masks and vehicles

The Five Branches which, for general definition, we have termed Warrior, Poet, Prophet, Priest, and King, are by no means the only harmonics of male entity, but are those which have very specific transformative functions, inner and outer skills, and training techniques for crossing psychic, magical, and spiritual thresholds toward empowerment and enlightenment. Initially, we can examine the relationship of the Five Branches to one another, and their collective relationship to the god-within, the Bright One.

First, we must distinguish between the specific and relative occupations expressed through or by these Branches, and the inner reality which they embody. More simply, we need to be aware that each of the Five Branches does not imply a hard and fast occupation or, in the modem definition, a psychological type, but acts initially as a mirror, and later will act as a clarifying lens.

Not all poets write or declaim verses, not all warriors defend or kill their fellow men and women, and not all priests mediate true spiritual power. Analogies of mirror and lens are used frequently in magical and spiritual training, as they embody the properties of light/energy that are either reflected or transmitted.

The images or god-forms that represent the Five Branches are first used in visualization as ideal figures, as mirrors in which we perceive truths apart from our self-image. At a later stage we turn around, making a complete change of consciousness and direction of attention and energy, and the idealized entity, the image or god-form, becomes transparent within ourselves, now acting as a lens rather than as a mirror. Before this major transition there are various intermediary stages and techniques by which we mediate the male images and their energies through ourselves. The mediation process clarifies our own inner energies and sets them in certain harmonic resonant patterns, thus creating and subsequently un-clouding the lens.

This model, which is more than a mere analogy, can be further developed in terms of the persona or mask, which is often, at first, a cracked or cloudy mirror, sometimes seeming to be an insurmountable barrier, but later transformed and rendered transparent to truly mediate that which is within. Modern society is increasingly fraught with problems for individuals in occupations that bear little or no relationship to their personalities, or indeed to any enduring sense of value. This type of separation becomes highly amplified when we move to those levels beyond the personality, and consider the inner Mysteries or spiritual depths of energy and consciousness. Our current culture has very little to offer men, or women, that fulfills or expresses their deepest inner patterns and realities.

In an idealized society, and perhaps, as we might assume, in simple cultures of the ancestral past (which may or may not have truly existed as we envisage them), the inner nature of a man was directly channeled and expressed by his occupation. A warrior took arms because his inner nature was that of the warrior, and so forth. Such primal situations are extremely powerful, for each individual expresses his potent inner energies directly. The persona or mask does not, in such cases, block or deflect the inner nature; rather, it acts as a harmonious filter, lens, or outer presentation for that which is within. To remove such a mask is merely to reveal the higher octave or level of energy that exists within or behind its appearance.

Some of this simple resonance was defined, in past cultures, by what are nowadays recognized (retrospectively) as caste systems; we should make a firm distinction between caste as a tool of oppression and slavery, and caste or collective groupings as a mutually acknowledged vehicle for skills interacting within a community. Some primal cultures today still have hereditary musicians, poets, warriors, and so forth, though this type of holism is rapidly fading from our world, and can often be antagonistic to modern paradigms. A contemporary scientist might think that there is a genetic predisposition among certain families for certain skills. Whereas an esotericist might suggest that skilled men choose to reincarnate within a certain bloodline and grouping, which enables them best to serve their tribe and land or environment. Both statements imply something similar; two viewpoints of truth that may be defined in different ways according to the conceptual and analytic model that we prefer.

The esoteric traditions, however, provide many insights and techniques for awakening awareness and bringing inner change, which are not found elsewhere; furthermore, if we limit ourselves to a materialist model, we often cannot access those other levels of awareness, for much of inner development depends crucially upon the imaginative forces. These forces, of themselves, arouse our various levels of energy to thresholds and levels that cannot be obtained through other means. The harmonic concept of the personality, as described above, differs from psychological or therapeutic theories of today.

The Five Branches and skills or crafts

There are Five Branches of the Male Mysteries, each of which will be discussed shortly. They consist of what we might call, in the terminology of an earlier culture, *noble* categories or classes. There is no suggestion of class snobbism or elitism, and no hint of meritocratic separation in this terminology. The word noble is used in its proper sense, for the Five Branches purify and ennoble the mind, the emotions, the soul. As in Tarot and chess—both ancient magical conceptual structures—the highest and lowest entities or units, the King and Fool, are identical, for both are the page/pawn/primal man who becomes ennobled. Such ennoblement comes in many ways; the way of the Male Mysteries is through conscious effort, working with forms in meditation, vision, and ceremony.

When we work within the perennial spiritual or transformative traditions, regardless of which Branch of the Mysteries we employ, much of the content is handed down from earlier cultures and civilizations; thus, there can be a tendency in modern men toward romantic escapism. Escapism can be avoided by working with defined methods rather than idealizing any one culture or era. The Western Esoteric Tradition is also called the Perennial Tradition, for it regenerates through the centuries, surfacing according to need.

Many of the images and concepts in general magical arts, for example, derive from the medieval period and, especially, the Renaissance, while much of the deeper mythic material derives from Greek, Celtic, Scandinavian, and other primal cultures. The higher technology of magic, in the forms of methods and specific systems, derives from Babylonian, Egyptian and, according to persistent widespread though unproven tradition, Atlantean civilizations. Thus there are a number of conceptual models, technical styles and vocabularies, generally preserved (often in a confused state) within the Mysteries and esoteric traditions as we find them today.

In addition to all of the foregoing, there is the important but often ignored collective or folk tradition of initiation, which involves ancestral and fairy/spirit beings, and the relationship between humanity and the land. This may partake of the more defined or recorded textual streams of tradition, but is often a powerful substratum that works almost independently of dominant cultures or civilizations.

The old cultural models, psychologies, mythologies, and cosmologies, require careful assessment and consideration by the modern man and woman. In many cases they act as invaluable correctives to our impoverished, coagulated life conditions and our corrupt, self-destructive culture. But their corrective power must be found upon inner levels, not outwardly. If we try to live the old cultural or social hieratic or religious systems outwardly, we may create situations of almost irresolvable conflict, hostility, and confusion.

There might seem, superficially, to be a rather good case for starting splinter groups or communes living according to old models of life, but this would be a negative step to take. Just as we are upon a new spiral or turning in human development, so must the patterns represented by the old cultures, often embodied within the esoteric traditions, be accessed and activated upon a new spiral, of the inner imaginative or spiritual dimensions. The old cultures made mistakes, just as we are making drastic mistakes, and to materialize them even in miniature is to call up ancient human errors. Upon a higher octave, however, we can merge the best of the old cultures with the seeds of a new pattern for the future. This comprises the essential continuity of tradition, not in outer forms and rigid customs, but upon inner levels which flow and remold themselves with each century. As mentioned above, the Five Branches all work upon and through the normal man, the raw material, the Earth of our Being.

This central and circumferential entity, the Man, the Worker, is not only what we are, but what we might be, and all that we ever have been. Thus, a number of initiatory and visionary exercises, particularly those concerned with learning from inner-world teachers, depend upon images of skill and craft, of what were once termed making and shaping.

Appendix 2 is a typical visualization to put us into contact with a certain type of imaginal or inner-world teacher. Such mentors are men of skill or of craft, not obviously belonging to one of the Noble Branches. But the effect of such inner-world mentors is very powerful indeed, though not always in the way that we might expect. Most of these inner-world teachers tend to be associated with skills or crafts that are no longer used today—the secret lore of animals, the skills of the woodsman, the worker in stone or metal using very simple non-technological tools and methods, the navigator who uses the stars, the gardener, and so forth. They should not be romanticized, for our entire evolution on Planet Earth was, and still is, generated by these skills.

Some teachers, encountered during meditation and guided visualization, are similar to those ancestors and mentors of humanity presented in primal myth and legend. But we need not rigidly identify them with such mythic beings, or assume that they are archetypes in the modern sense of the word. Some inner-world teachers are certainly of a collective mythic nature, but others seem to be highly individual, and difficult to label by any generalized definition. In terms of survival, we do not seem to need such ancient skills today; no matter how romantic or idealistic we may be, it must be admitted that most of us cannot live in a manner approaching that embodied by these ancestral archetypical or inner-world teachers.

Skills and crafts revisited

What, therefore, do we learn? While it is possible to learn specific skills and techniques from inner-world teachers, their main gift to us is one of wisdom, understanding, and insight. This is a subtle subject, hard to put into words, for much depends upon actual contact and experience. Work with inner-world teachers of skill and craft is greatly enhanced by practical work in or approximating to the traditional skill that they represent.

There is an ancient and accepted rule in magical arts,[18] which is that an initiate should never make his or her living by selling magical services. The actual living is supposed to be made with the hands, through a practical skill or craft. This is not some type of inverted snobbery or dark secrecy for anonymity, but an eminently practical rule. Only through a skill can certain forces manifest properly, and it is essential for the meditator, visualizer, seer, magician, or whatever we care to call ourselves, to have a physical vehicle for his or her abilities.

The Branch or way of the Priest

The priest is one of the most ancient and in many ways least changing Branches of the Male Mysteries, just as priestess is within the Women's Mysteries. We are not referring to priest as social worker, confessor, moral or political activist, charity worker, counselor, and so forth. True priesthood is defined by a perennial and unchanging ability to mediate spiritual forces, with well-defined disciplines, roles, obligations, and orders or initiatory lines of succession.

Priests are usually born with an inherent priestly ability, and it cannot be simply trained into a man in one lifetime. Crossing into the Branch of priesthood is not usually made by sudden leaps in one lifetime as are changes of role in the other major Branches of the Mystery. If we do not have the priestly ability from birth, we may acquire it through gradual inner transformation, to be born with in a subsequent life. The sudden revelation or blinding vision, often associated with emotional conversions to a standard religion or with entering the formal orders of an orthodox priesthood, may or may not be a true religious experience. Either way, it does not mean that the person undergoing the experience is suddenly a priest, merely that he has had an unusual vision.

Many men have latent priestly abilities which they choose to ignore, or which are deeply buried by the dross and pollution of our contemporary way of life. Let us consider how such a priestly nature might manifest itself today.

The priest is essentially someone who, sometimes despite himself, is able to mediate and bring through divine power, the contact of a higher octave of consciousness, or of a god or goddess-form or entity. That is all there is to priesthood, an inborn ability to mediate spiritual power. The rest comes with dedication, discipline, and devotion. Like any other talent, we either can or cannot do it. If we choose to be a priest, founded upon this innate ability, we may then develop and refine it.[19]

Many lines of priesthood are genetic, descending through family bloodlines over long periods of time. Such genetic lines of priesthood from ancient times tend to mediate very specific god- or goddess-forms; yet this inherited starting point can develop into an ability to mediate any god or goddess, any subtle energy, or spiritual power. If we remain undeveloped, we can become atavistic. This tendency wrapped up in atavism is a negative male attribute, well represented in our seemingly modernist society.

The important exception to this old genetic tendency is the line or order of Sacred Kings, typified in Judaism and Christianity by the little-understood figure of Melchizedek in the Old Testament. This line of priesthood cuts across familial and racial boundaries; it is one of three higher octaves of priesthood, merging with and arising from the inner Kingship, the last threshold before encountering the Source of Being directly.

Priesthood is associated with the higher centers of energy and consciousness, though it may be an innate or even involuntary or unconscious ability in some men. Thus it is located in the head (see Figure 6), or in some traditional teachings slightly above the physical head of the individual. It is the originating and unifying power for the Right and Left Hand, the Poet and Warrior. There is a general correspondence of this ancient polarity teaching to modern research into the activities and functions of the right and left hemispheres of the brain.

The Branch or way of the Poet

The term poet is used here in its oldest sense, quite different from our modern notion of poets, which seems to include all kinds of humorous entertainers who might originally never have been considered poets. The poet is used here to mean the creative individual who makes forms by combining words and images into expressed patterns that have a powerful effect upon the listener or reader. In this category we might therefore include music, for the primal poets were bardic, using images and music fused together in their art. The way of the poet, in its broadest sense, is the way of creative discipline, rendering form out of energy, and preserving and communicating that form. It might be as visual art, music, words, or even as dance and movement.

There are many interactions between the Five Branches, and no man is solely of one type or of one Branch. The dancer and the warrior, for example, are very closely related. Both involve great skill, determination, discipline, and above all, highly trained and developed physical coordination. The dancer and the warrior share something subtle together too, for both cross thresholds and cause others to cross thresholds through their body movements.

In ancient times the poet was a combination of musician and creator of verses as originally written poetry did not exist. There is a typical modern delusion that such ancient poets were crude folksy rhymesters, and modern men occasionally go through a simplistic phase of poetry in which they try to ape this utterly spurious simplicity, a type of poetry that never existed in the first place. There are a few remarkable exceptions to this, which are not the product of modern sentiment.

The primal poet and bard was a man to be feared and respected. The power of making and unmaking was in his breast and upon his tongue. So few modern poets come anywhere near this terrifying threshold, that we might be excused for wondering if the power of poetry has almost abandoned our world. But of course it has not, and though it might be overlaid with experiment and innovation, poetry will not abandon us.

In the individual the power of the poet is traditionally that of the left hand the artistic and imaginative qualities of a man (see Figures 5 and 6). The left hand is the area or energy of the feminine forces of the male psyche. In mystical or divine attributes upon the Tree of Life (Figure 2), the left hand pillar is feminine, flowing from the Great Goddess, while the right hand is masculine, uttered by the God. This polarity pattern was recognized and used in meditation and spiritual training many centuries before modern theories of animus, anima, or right and left brain potentials were formulated.

The Branch or way of the Prophet

While the Poet is both the memory and inspirer of his people, the Prophet is the conscience. It is often assumed, quite wrongly, that prophets are solely concerned with foretelling the future; this is only one aspect of prophetic consciousness.[20]

It seems that prophets, in a strict definition of the term, are almost without exception male. We must exercise caution with such conclusions, however, as history has been heavily doctored and twisted by orthodox male-dominated religion for many centuries. The sibyls, or female prophets, of the ancient world seem to have worked in a different way from their male counterparts. A difference which we will examine shortly, and which may be due to those polarities of physical gender which make specific changes and definitions of inner energies whenever such energies manifest. The energies may be identical, but they may manifest in different forms according to the gender of the human prophet or sybil.

None of the foregoing implies any stereotypical roles or inflexible sets of laws. Furthermore, the boundaries, thresholds and exchanges between male and female are fluid, changing through the ages both collectively and individually. Such changes tend to be very slow and long term, and we are in a particularly difficult position to judge them at present due to the confusion resulting from a long period of imbalance that has harmed men and women through an over-emphasis on totally false "masculine" qualities.

One thing is certain, there are clear indications of a change of collective and individual awareness at present. It seems to be reaching toward a higher octave or spiral of a period which slowly came to an end about 3,000 years ago, when most human societies were still, broadly speaking, matrifocal, as shown by the fact that the Great Goddess was the ultimate aspect of divinity then identified by humanity. The last 1,500 years of militant, dogmatic, political, Christianity in the West, is the final manifestation of forces that tended to destroy the older Goddess orientated cultures and replace them with those in which men claimed an innate superiority. This final manifestation now includes rampant materialism and fervent scientism.

The male prophet often sees that which is ignored by most other men, feels the impending disasters that may be averted, and makes painful but direct contact with other states of Being, particularly those which humanity calls either Underworld or Divine. He does not do this solely through intuition, but through a different rate or faculty of consciousness, which may manifest through intuition, intellect, emotion, or through what are nowadays obscure techniques and symbolic structures of communication. If we consider the ancient world briefly, we find that sybils tended toward divine possession or mantic trances, in which the presence of a god or goddess fills the priestess (sybil) and takes over her regular persona, suppressing it entirely. This is similar in some ways to modern mediumship or channeling, but it must be stressed that the presence of a god or goddess in a human body is a different degree of power to the familiar presence of most "spirit guides."

In the Celtic and Classical cultures, as in some primal rites today, the presence of the god in a human form was a terrifying experience, not to be taken lightly, and was always clearly understood to be different from the communication of spirits, ancestors, heroes, and other lesser entities.

The male prophet, however, tends not to be a physical vehicle for a god or goddess-form, but to make some kind of connection to the deity or power concerned without displacement or total suppression of individuality. The names, types, or definitions of deity are irrelevant in such circumstances, for the vision of the God or Goddess is, thankfully perhaps, always filtered through a cultural environment and racial set of symbols and beliefs. Though there is a vast amount of active propaganda concerning orthodox, politically enforced gods and their much-vaunted universality, they are still clearly racial and local in their history, origin, and behavior.

A small number of mystics and visionaries, however, can gain access to a degree of universal consciousness and Being by reaching through and beyond these flawed local daemons that pass themselves off as universal omnipotent gods or God Himself. It is well worth noting in this context that only a few of the ancient gods claim universality or omnipotence. Many of these claims to universality arise not from the deities, but from their priesthood laying claim to authority.

The simplicity of god-forms is often thought to be due to their assumedly primitive limited nature, and to the lack of development of those people who worshipped them. Yet specific god-forms are extremely powerful and can be of enormous benefit to the development of human beings, without ever claiming universality. This situation is central to the Male Mysteries and will repay much meditation. Male imbalance as we know it today, as it manifests in myriad forms throughout our Western world, was considerably accelerated as the result of a simple tribal god being declared universal, and ultimately having his worship enforced at the point of a sword.

Aggressive monotheism is a very effective tool of suppression indeed, for all the many images and energies which were inherently transformative and liberating were suddenly "lesser," or even "evil," and thus could be banned, perverted, expunged, ignored.

The prophet is one of those few chosen men who are not a superior or elite brotherhood, but considered by many (including themselves sometimes) as accursed and mad. In a man, the prophetic consciousness is uncontrollable and comes and goes as it will. He is often driven temporarily mad by such visions and by the opening of his perception to human pain and suffering.

Regrettably, the way of the prophet is also one by which dangerous delusions of glamour and grandeur can overtake a man's ego and ultimately destroy him. Many weak men choose to pretend to be prophets, and can eventually convince many, even themselves. They do not need the skill and discipline of the warrior, or the training and artistic talent of the poet, to support their claim. Prophecy, like New Age channeling and spiritual mastery or so-called immortality, has long been replete with frauds, charlatans and deluded naive individuals. The true prophet is known by one particular hallmark—he is almost always unwilling to receive his prophetic gifts and transcendent or trans-temporal understanding. A very small number of prophets come to terms with their talent, and may mature through it and be able to cope with it. In many men, the prophetic energies wane after a certain age—the onset is usually puberty and the waning period is often in the mid-30s. Prophecy is closely linked to sexuality and polarity.

We need not presume that the prophet is totally filled with cosmic insights; he is the young man who sees the evil of war and makes his protest felt, wondering why all those around him cannot see and are opposed to his opposition. He is the campaigner for the environment, the man who withdraws from the social and economic struggle, not because he fails, but because he sees beyond the spurious values and the complex strands of enslavement that such a struggle involves. More rarely nowadays, he is the visionary man of politics, but this type of prophet should be regarded with extreme caution, as it is one of the most likely areas to be filled with ego, fraud, deceit, and delusion.

Traditionally we find that prophets were often also warriors or poets, and there is a direct transition from warrior or poet to prophet within every man. It comes through pain and hardship, and is often catalyzed by compassion for the suffering of others.

In the individual man, prophecy is associated with the genitals, the Lunar center, and the mysterious Underworld. When a prophet is inflamed with inspiration, the sexual energies rise up to the solar or king center (see Figure 6). Under specific circumstances and with training, the energies will rise into the head center. The reflex or polarity between Prophet and Priest is that the Underworld energies are spontaneously uttered through the mouth of the Prophet. In simpler terms we have all experienced this, for it occurs as the sudden truth that we blurt out unwittingly.

The Branch or way of the Warrior

The Warrior is the most popular, visible, obvious, yet most frequently confused Branch of the Male Mysteries. Much of this confusion in popular imagination arises from a single-sided development of the warrior image, usually with false emphasis placed upon physical attributes and skill at violence.

More space has been given to the Branch of Warrior simply because this seems to be the most prevalent Branch in modern man, either in fact, or in terms of valid or invalid aspirations. The Warrior is traditionally associated with the right hand (see Figures 5 and 6) powers of strength, reason, physical development and so forth. He needs to be balanced by the left hand of the poet. At later stages of development he may consciously relate to the central or spinal Branches of King, Prophet, and Priest.

In an ideal or idealized society, where people seem to have well-defined interacting roles, the warrior group, caste, or class is often held in balance by other groups through their functions. The individual warrior finds harmony for his outgoing and dynamic energies through such interactions and relationships, which are often non-personal and non-sexual. One of the problems in modern practice is that as soon as we use words like "relationship" there is a tendency toward a sexual connotation. This is due to centuries of sexual repression and imbalance, as a result of which we place a vast over-emphasis upon the role of physical gratification and emotional attachment, both of which are somewhat superficial levels of relationship and sexuality.

At this superficial or outermost level, the suppressive and enervating stereotypes of sexuality and sexual roles come into play, and we need to destroy such stereotypes forever. This task is, in itself, one for strong and persistent skilled warriors to undertake. In the earliest ideal societies or cultures, of course, warriors were not exclusively male; contemporary archaeology is increasingly identifying warrior burials as those of both men and women.

Our idealized ancestral societies, held together by transpersonal concepts and spiritual values, do not, of course exist today, if indeed they ever existed. Nevertheless, we can look to models of idealized societies or images from history to give us insight and inspiration concerning the roles of the Five Branches. On an inner level the personal balance of a warrior is gained through a combination of action and stillness; such techniques are still widely taught in martial arts. Far less well known, however, and less publicized, are the powerful techniques, once practiced in Western culture, for the spiritual warrior. Regrettably, politics and religion have shrouded this important Branch of the Male Mysteries in ignorance and delusion.

Perhaps the best-known Western examples presenting such techniques, albeit in a rather rarefied literary form, are the early texts concerning the court of King Arthur, the orders of knighthood, and the Quest for the Holy Grail. These often mask a pre-Christian tradition of the spiritual warrior, rooted in Celtic and early European history and myth. To a lesser extent we also find such techniques in the Classical myths of the Greek and Roman worlds, though these have suffered much through repeated editing and misinterpretation, much of it intentional, over the centuries.

The Warrior and the ideal or model society

The ideal society, aspired toward, dreamed of, or, more rarely, deliberately used in meditation and inner vision, also acts in many ways as a model for individual and social or group maturity. It works in a very direct and simple way, through personal or collective development of those qualities represented by the personae or roles found within that model society. One of the best-known models of this sort was that of the perfect spiritual city in which the Grail is found. Sacred cities in legend or vision, are models of balance and grace, in the center of which is always a valuable spiritual truth or object.

Philosophers have sought to intellectually define such perfect cultures or social entities, as in Plato's Republic, while at the other extreme of consciousness, mystics and visionaries perceive such perfected places instantly in fits of inspiration, joy, and terror. As with all such images, there can be an inversion or perversion—the shadow image. The concept of the elitist heaven or heavenly city into which the elect are gathered while the rest of us are consigned to hell, is one obvious example of such corruption and manipulation of a mythic image toward suppressive ends.

The technique of envisioning and working toward the ideal culture or society was widely used in mystical and magical training, and in many cases the imagery attuned to real entities, real cultures, actual worlds, and dimensions. Nowadays, we tend to take a more psychological approach to this type of developing model, and so lose much of the power inherent in the ancient methods, which were never confined to a purely mental or emotional level, but had the potential to bridge between the human awareness and that of other entities in other states of existence. Even if we set this important aspect of the perennial traditions aside, there is still great potential in these ideal images of people within idealized social and physical structures.

One subtle operative function is that of the physical structure, its proportions, its allocation of the Four Directions and so forth. Spiritual or magical cities, lands, zones, and structures are seldom random. Originally, people intentionally but naturally reflected this holistic pattern making—which attuned both human and geomantic forces—in the actual structure of their cities and the harmonic areas or divisions of the land. Thus in ancient Ireland or Ancient Greece, we find that certain zones, directions, or tribes, are specifically those of the warriors, musicians, poets, magicians, and so forth.

The allocation of the Directions is discussed in Chapter 6 and shown in Figure 1.

The Warrior and the Grail

In Western culture we find the role of the warrior and hero highly emphasized in history from ancient times. In modern history, the soldier or hero takes on a very political role, and in most recent times is regarded, at worst, as a creature of futility and degradation, the professional killer and suppressor of the weak, and at best as an innocent victim of unscrupulous manipulators, who send young men to die in vast numbers for false causes, with secret purposes of aggrandizement profit and personal power being crudely masked by patriotism, religion, and political jargon.

But at one time the role of warrior and hero (hero being a concise term rather than a general word of praise) merged with that of the Sacred King. The warrior who dies in certain circumstances may become absorbed into the Branch of the Sacrificial Kingship. In such circumstances, his death frees him from the imbalances of his life, and purifies his spirit, through his dedication to the benefit of the people for whom he dies. This is, nowadays, an obscure and often misunderstood concept, one which may be easily abused by propagandists and unscrupulous manipulators: it reappears in many contexts in the Male Mysteries.

The Warrior is the Branch suited to the physically active, fit, and generally outgoing individual. But this is merely the initial stage of the path, often entered into during youth. It seems a terrible fate that our modern men of great physical skill, such as sportsmen, only have a short working life. They become highly over-developed for a few years, in the hope of earning vast sums of money: but after the first phase of their life (from youth into adulthood, see Figure 1), they are already discarded, outlived, burned up. This elite level of the problem is reflected generally in many young men who go through a phase of physical skills, only to lose such interest and fitness in their late 20s or 30s, and to become sluggish and immovable once the obvious vigor of youthful sport has, apparently, left them.

The true development of the Warrior, however, is clearly indicated in the wisdom traditions of both East and West. Physical skills and honorable martial abilities, developed through long training, are all aimed at a transformation of consciousness. The reason why our modern sportsmen and highly physically skilled men, or indeed the youthful sportsman who becomes a sluggish adult, all fail to develop beyond a certain age, is nothing to do with physical degeneration or aging itself. The problem is that the attitude and training is all directed outwardly—skill to gain praise, skill to earn money.

The warrior training of earlier cultures was certainly aimed at building skills, and to develop young men into skilled fighters and defenders, but it had many deeper levels which persisted and developed through the entire lifetime. A true warrior never retires, but moves the development of skill and understanding inwards, until he achieves harmony by unifying the warring aspects of his self: this then becomes the state of inner Kingship through which the Bright One, the inner divinity, may at last appear.

In the Grail legends we find this traditional training and aspiration stated in a curious fusion of pagan and Christian lore.[21] The knight, the warrior, with his vigor and skill at arms, must give up seeking military glory, and so quest after the unattainable. The Grail, seen at first as a physical vessel or treasure, is found to be a spiritual condition; yet it is associated with the Celestial City attuned to the geomantic power place on Earth, and has a true physical and metaphysical existence in its own right. In other words, it is not what we moderns would call "a state of mind" or what the orthodox religious might have called "a state of grace." These merely help the aspirant to perceive or make brief contact with the Grail. Preparation for this inner revelation is not only in physical skills, but in the ethical and spiritual rules absorbed by the warrior. Let us examine these briefly, for they are central to the Male Mysteries in any form, at any time, in any place or world.

The warrior is under many strict rules, all ultimately leading to a sense of true responsibility. He and he alone is responsible for the outcome of his actions. The physical skills are dependent upon long hours of practice, until the coordination, the harmony of body and mind, lead to a fusion of vital energies and consciousness, giving a transpersonal or spiritual experience, an initiation of higher consciousness. This comes through perfect motion, impersonal skill, a state of pure being that may be attained through physical development combined with meditation. Many other skills involving movement relate to this.

The strength and skill of the warrior are kept from overspilling into random action through a set of simple but potent rules: he must defend the weak; he must use his power and skill only to beneficial ends; he must be able not merely to control his emotions, but to transmute them, to be aware and alert in inner states beyond emotion. In early training, these qualities are reinforced by vows, by rules, by the presence and advice and, if necessary, admonition, of senior mature men. In the case of the ancient Irish warriors, the training was often carried out by warrior women, a subject which is described in detail in the legend of Cuchulainn, an invaluable source of material for the Male Mysteries.

Through meditation and proper training, the ethical and spiritual values become more than mere conditioning, for the warrior gains insights into truth, into relative conditions of reality. He understands that the stronger and more powerful an individual or group becomes, the more such power must be guided by compassion, by non-selfish ends, by service to the community, the tribe, the nation, and ultimately to all humankind.

This deep transformation is found in Western tradition in the courtly and knighthood rules, well known to us from medieval and later literature. The fact that such rules were greatly abused and ignored, even while giving lip service to them, does not alter the validity of the code itself. Just as there are weak and cowardly bullies and monsters in every age, so are there always a number of true warriors, perfect knights. Ultimately the warrior must be willing to die to protect the people: this is the same ethic of compassion and non-personality that is at the heart of non-violent ways such as Buddhism. It is interesting to consider this context, that many warrior skills are found in a non-violent context. The same concepts are hidden deep within the knightly code of the West, which derives from the warrior code of the ancient Celts and Greeks.

If we delve far back into the world of our ancestors, we find a very different attitude to life and death than ours today. In the Christian era the warrior or knight was often encouraged to meditate upon death, a meditation with spiritual origins that gradually became linked to its own shadow within orthodox religion.

Such political/militaristic religious conditioning often led to terrible results; the murder of non-believers and the persecution of other races. The knightly code, however, aimed to transcend physical death, to show how irrelevant it is. And little wonder, for the knightly code is founded directly upon the heroic warrior code of an earlier world, exemplified by the Celtic and Greek heroes. These warrior codes were originally rooted in a matrifocal goddess-worshipping culture; we frequently find that the warrior training and spiritual inspiration was under the control of women, both as human, superhuman and divine beings.

The most terrifying goddesses of the ancient world were often warrior goddesses; we should be cautious about embracing modern divisive scenarios which say that patriarchal militaristic men destroyed the old goddess culture. The evidence of warrior goddesses, fusing the powers of life, sexuality and death, inspiring and training heroes, warriors, and prophets and poets, is clear from early cultures. Thus no one who has truly examined what we know of such cultures can claim that they became divisive, with aggressive men eventually destroying the non-aggressive goddess civilization either from within or from without. As with all difficult evolutionary change, the pendulum swings slowly, slowly, until we suddenly discover that has left old patterns behind and is ushering in new ones. Then it swings again.

The concept of ancient male aggression toward the Goddess seems likely to be a retrospective attribute; it echoes the propaganda that a monotheistic focus is better than other forms of religion. The great goddesses of sexuality and death, such as the Irish Morrigan, the mythic warrior women who trained young men, such as the Scottish Schathach (who gives her name to the Isle of Skye), and the Classical goddesses of war and cultural development, wisdom and knowledge, such as Minerva or Athena, were not divinities of aggression. Indeed the developing image of this group of goddesses, very central to the Male Mysteries, reaches from a savage but impersonal goddess of life and death within the sacred land, to a calm and wise goddess (Athena). She mediated the primal, powerful warrior skills and forces, attuning them as she wished, including the direct protection, education and initiation of chosen men.

For modern use we may, with some caution but also with powerful results, turn to the earlier code of warrior conduct embedded within the Classical and Celtic myths that tell of such goddesses and their chosen male trainees, initiates, or heroes. There are a number of reasons why the world-view of a very early culture may be valid today. On the more obvious levels we find that it bypasses the corrupt areas of political religion, often acting as shock treatment to jolt us out of our materialist complacency, a complacency sitting uncomfortably on the surface of deep unrest and confusion. Second, the passage of cultural or collective growth is not a straight line but a complex of inter-linked spirals. More simply, we are at a turning point similar to that of 2,000 years ago, the threshold between the pagan and Christian eras in the West. It is possible to tap into the energies and primal concepts of our ancestors through the law of octaves: we are now where they were, but at a different harmonic or octave level. The primal attitude to life, death, battle, and warrior skills, is central to the development of modern men: otherwise, we are returning to deadening and vicious traps that we found when we entered this life.

The Warrior as hero

Heroes play a large part in the mythology and legendary history of our world. In recent years it has become fashionable to laugh at the hero, and in modern film and fiction to delight in the anti-hero; we have seen through the false hero, but may not yet have recovered the true hero. The false hero is the sexual all-male stereotype with bulging muscles, jutting jaw, all decision, action, and little or no emotion or introspection. These types frequently appear in early films: gentlemen detectives, war heroes and so forth. They also dominate much of early 20th century popular fiction. We may rapidly set such images aside ... they are a dead end. Primal heroes, however, are a different matter. They embody certain strengths and weaknesses that are inherent in every male. Many of their legends reveal much to us concerning initiation, spiritual growth, emotional maturity, and humankind's relationship to both environmental and apparently supernatural forces. Many heroes are the sons of divine beings, often of a union between one human parent and one divine. Such unions reveal a great deal of information on ancient methods of initiation and transformation ... they are not mere allegories or superstitions.

In modern terms, we may look at the inherent character of the hero through the ages; certain persistent fundamental qualities and actions define a hero ... even down to our modern stereotypes who pale into insignificance beside their ancestral counterparts.

What makes a hero?

A hero is a warrior of some sort, usually but not inevitably, a trained fighter, bearer of arms. There are, of course, heroes who never lift a weapon or fight a physical battle. Their heroic deeds are, nevertheless, still definable. The hero has certain strengths, be they of muscle or will, brain or body. But he is also unfailingly motivated by gentleness and compassion, without which he is merely an unfeeling thug or a soldier pawn in the hands of unscrupulous manipulators. He protects the weak, assists them, and will, if necessary, sacrifice his own interests, even his life, to protect defend and benefit others.

These qualities are all essentially nurturing; they are those of the mother ... feminine qualities. The hero is not a superman; he is a highly empowered active dynamic male whose maleness is balanced by feminine qualities, feelings, and abilities.

In some legends, we find this truth exemplified by the relationship between a hero and a goddess. The Irish hero Cuchulainn,[22] for example, has astonishing powers, skills, strength, energy, sexual prowess, beauty, and so forth. But he fails to acknowledge that a major part of his potential is through the blessing and protection of the Morrigan, the primal goddess of sexuality and death. Because he fails to recognize her, both literally during several meetings, and of course inwardly, she eventually withdraws her blessing and protection. Through his failure to identify the goddess, Cuchulainn loses much of his supernatural strength and skill, and so may be killed by his enemies.

This theme recurs frequently in the Arthurian and Grail legends of later medieval literature: the feminine qualities, the mysterious powers of the goddess, are essential for the king, the knight, the hero. Without them he is incomplete, a one-sided stereotype. The sword Excalibur is nothing without the Scabbard: Arthur is weakened and destroyed without Guinevere, and so forth. We might take this today as a reminder that the right hand (the sword hand of the Warrior) is imbalanced without the left hand (the scabbard-hand of the feminine, shown as the Branch of the Poet). There is another suggestive paradox: the Right Hand and the Left Hand interchange. The right hand is the sword hand of severity, yet severity is upon the left hand pillar of the Tree of Life. The left hand is the hand of mercy, yet mercy is on the right hand pillar of the Tree. It all depends on this: are we looking at the Tree, facing it from without, or are we within it. Right and Left interchange ceaselessly in the turning of the Wheel.[23]

CHAPTER 6

The Worker and the Wheel of Life

The Worker—his skills and crafts

The Five Branches pattern used in this book is not, of course, the only possible model that might define masculine entities, roles, and related energies or states of consciousness. Environmentally defined and balanced systems were well known in early cultures, depending upon caste (in a non-elitist sense), occupation, and, interestingly, geographical or spatial location. Early societies orientated their settlements, cities, territories and lands according to Sacred Directions and geomantic locations; specific castes or occupations were often located in specific Quarters or Directions.

A typical example is ancestral Ireland, with the royal court in the center of the land, and the various castes or occupations laid out according to the Sacred Directions of East, South, West, and North. This spatial pattern has its inner or metaphysical geometry, for the Directions corresponded to the Four Elements of Air, Fire, Water, and Earth, and to the four seasons of Spring, Summer, Autumn, and Winter. This fourfold Elemental pattern is found in a developed expression in the

Tarot, where the personae or Court Cards correspond to certain relative human types, interacting in an Elemental relationship to one another (see Figure 1). On a deeper level, the human Elemental personae become archetypes or primal god- and goddess-forms. Tarot is merely one example of a highly developed psychology pre-dating materialist models of the psyche such as we have today. In an inversion of standards, modern psychology "explains" these earlier models, as if they are not effective or comprehensive in their own right.

Our four major Branches of Warrior, Poet, Prophet, and Priest are male archetypes or inner-world forms for specific energies. They actually stand at the Cross-Quarters of the Circle: we might begin with the Warrior in the South East, the Poet in the South West, the Prophet in the North West, and the Priest in the North East. In the center is the King.

The positions suggested are not rigid or dogmatic, and in visionary practices and special ceremonial or ritual pattern making, we may find that they change position. The overall pattern described (as shown in Figure 6) is the basic set of relationships of the Five Branches or Beings. Seasonal attributes are very important in this context, and the relationships and harmonies or polarities should always be linked to the concept of Sacred Space and the Wheel of Life (as in Figure 1).

Lists of correspondences are fruitless without an overview or unifying model, such as that of Sacred Space and the Wheel of Life. The seasons combine the phases of energy in the land (due to planetary orbit and rotation relative to the Sun) with the phases of birth, adulthood, maturity, and old age in a human being. When we work with such holistic models, they slowly transform all levels of our perception, and generate a deep sense of connection and rhythm between every aspect of life within and around us.

The seemingly missing person in our structure of relative male archetypes is of course, the basic man, the Worker. Originally he would have been the peasant, laborer, farmer, huntsman, or craftsman. The worker group also has within itself a fourfold or multifold spiral of directions and relationships. Holistic structures and patterns mirror the whole within each part. In the Male Mysteries, the worker, the laborer, the basic man, is of course ourselves. Thus he is the simplest level of male entity, but also the most complex and all-inclusive. The King and the Worker or Peasant are one and the same person; the work is whatever we do within ourselves, moving toward transformation. Thus we are worker and work, material and craftsman.

Losing power

Let us now look at one of the most typical problems that men in general have today: loss of power and identity. What is there in the broad range of the Male Mysteries that can resolve situations, both inner and outer, that bring loss of power? The most significant areas in which the traditional male initiations and practices can work are the inner levels of being. Most males, unfortunately, are strongly dependent upon exterior circumstances for their sense of identity; when these circumstances are changed or disempowered, the man collapses. This situation is found in men of all abilities, social groups, and levels of power and intelligence. It applies as strongly and as terribly to the laboring man who loses his job as it does to the executive who is defeated in a boardroom struggle.

We find this sorry situation reflected in a much broader way in the emblems of the consumer society, in which we are all, male and female, encouraged to assess our worth by the objects which we own, by the image which we assemble through these objects, ranging from work, to home, to clothes, and body image. Reassurance is found, we are repeatedly told, by looking at the objects that we own, at the status that we have, at our face and body in the mirror, and seeing that they are good.

The levels of indoctrinated value are subtly in flux, for they are molded by the profit motive of entities, such as, but not solely limited to, those commercial ventures that sell us such images. The outer shell has, somehow, become the main focus of entity for men, and when it is broken, they often die. It is a simple truth that many men, upon retiring from dull, deadening, trivial, and utterly pointless work, in which they have remained for a major part of their life simply to scrape a living, will lie down, or more likely sit, and die. The reason for living, unfulfilling as it was, has been taken away from them. Many social and psychological studies of this phenomenon have been made, but it is really the most obvious expression of something that happens in every man repeatedly whenever he loses power or there is an exterior manifest reason for his existence.

Whenever a man loses power, loses an exterior focus, he dies. In the final case, he dies physically, but during his lifetime a man will die and be reborn a number of times.

This is a powerful feature of human energy and/or consciousness, male and female, but it manifests more distinctly in males. Women have a continuity and rhythm that men, at present, lack. A man tends to mature by fits and starts, while a woman tends to mature in a steady progression. Thus, if we take a theoretical man and theoretical woman, they might begin a life cycle at the same level of awareness. The woman is more likely to make rhythmic steady progress toward maturity and understanding: sometimes the man will be far behind the woman; at other theoretical points in time, he will have leaped ahead. This pattern is found again, in higher and lower octaves, upon the inner levels, with spiritual cycles of development, death, and rebirth. Men can make long leaps into the Unknown, but women are able to move steadily through a continuum, a holism, a pleroma, and reach the same mysterious destination.

Furthermore, for the male, it is literally the Unknown into which he leaps, but the female is able, to a certain extent, to sense what lies beyond such thresholds. This obscure sexual relationship was epitomized in the ancient sacrificial rites, in which a priestess officiated over the transfer, sending the male spirit into the otherworld. Some of this subject is covered in our chapter on the Sacred Kingship.

On a physical sexual level we find this transition manifesting through the male orgasm, which tends to be a single explosive event, while the woman is capable of repeated orgasms. The magical link between sexuality and death has been observed via psychology, but misconstrued, possibly reflecting the desires of the observers rather than any truth concerning human psychic energies and patterns.

On a metaphysical level, we find that gender or polarity is a matter of shape, just as it is upon the outermost physical manifestation, though there are many harmonics or levels in between. Metaphysics, and the perennial models used in metaphysics, magic, and mystical cosmology, and their related contemplative exercises, all affirm and rely upon certain primal universal patterns: beginning with the point, the line, and the circle. We still call this geometry (Earth-measure) today, after the Ancient Greek manner, but such sacred geometry has a universal expression and truth. Geometry means the measuring of the Earth, but the Earth or world concerned is not limited to the surface of our planet; it is the universal World, of which our two-dimensional geometry is merely a working analogy.

This inherent power within properties of shape is found again in the implements of magical ceremony, usually the sword, rod, cup, and shield, and the mobile shape of the cord. These are, in a pure shape sense, the line, the circle, and the surface. Such properties of shape and movement manifest in us as energies, as consciousness, and of course, as gender. The male shape is, outwardly, that of the rod or line, shown sexually by the penis. The female shape is, outwardly, that of the cup circle or spiral, shown sexually by the vulva. There is no suggestion here that these are limiting or all-inclusive stereotypes, merely that such universal shapes are relatively manifested through gender.

There is no question that men and women have both male and female shapes and energies within them, in the endless relative patterns and ramifications of humanity, and on to broader patterns within the holism of the land, the planet, the solar system, the universe. But the rod or line is only relative; the cup or vulva is only a relative shape within a fullness of other shapes, all mutually defining one another in a changing resonant flow. That linear leap made by a male when he dies and is reborn to a new level of awareness is in truth a spiral. That universal spiral of the Great Mother is, in truth, an infinitely long line, spiraling into a circular matrix.

These seemingly abstract truths are properties of energy, and are revealed today as relative laws or tendencies by our most advanced physics. Thus the scientific materialist levels of research have at last come a full circle, to confirm that which was always taught in the Mysteries. Now that science is destroying its very foundations of pseudo-masculine logic; men can begin to die and be reborn onto a new level of understanding.

The Wheel of Life and the Seven Directions

The Wheel of Life relates the Four Elements, the Seasons, the Directions, and various states of power to one another. It also relates through its ceaseless turning, the phases of a life cycle, both for gods and humans. Traditionally, certain images are located in certain Quarters of the Circle or Wheel. In Western magic, this concept is fundamental; and in magical and spiritual training worldwide, the concept of the Seven Directions occurs repeatedly. The Wheel (as we see in Figure 1) appears to have only Four Quarters, those of the East, South, West, and North. But it is a flat glyph or map completed by the presence of a human standing within it at the center. It is, in fact, a definition of our standing position and zone of awareness; thus, it represents the surface of the land or planet, and the sphere of awareness or being. This sphere ultimately embraces the universe, though most of us are content to settle for a sphere of awareness that is a little smaller.

The Seven Directions, then, are Above/Below, East/West, South/North, and Within. God-forms and images are related to each Direction. More traditionally, we would say that the gods are found in these Directions—that they dwell therein naturally. The Circle or Wheel and the Tree of Life are part of one another—the Tree grows in the center of the sphere—it is both the upright human with the stars above and the land below, and the Axis Mundi, or pivot of the worlds, through the center of the Solar System. (For Gods upon the Tree of Life, see Chapter 9.)

East

In the East, we find gods of Spring, change, turbulence, swiftly moving force. The Element is Air, which is both Breath of Spirit, and the howling hurricane of destruction. The gods of Air are frequently associated with warrior skills, and therefore have a further level of honor, protection of the weak, defense of the victim against the oppressor. Because Air is also the Element of communication, in terms of speech, music, and more subtly, consciousness or swiftly moving thoughts, we find messenger gods and teacher gods, and communicator gods in the Eastern Quarter. The techniques and forces of arousal, be it sexual or intellectual, are taught and enabled by the gods of the Eastern Quarter. The magical implement is the Sword or Arrow. The Inner Temple of the East is one of Instruction and Inspiration.

South

In the South, we find gods of ascension, of Summer, of Light, of balanced power. The Element is Fire, both in the form of the burning flame, the midsummer sun, and the universal power of Light. The gods of this Quarter maintain a balance and harmony of the fiery powers, and are concerned with therapy, enlightenment, and the harmony of inner forces. The forces that are aroused in the East are elevated and balanced in the South. In this Quarter, we find the gods of redemption, the great Saviors and enlighteners of humanity. We also find the midsummer gods of the land who bring the highest solar forces to bear upon the Earth within the turning of the wheel of the year. The implement of the South is the Rod or Staff. The Inner Temple of the South is one of Initiation and Illumination.

West

In the West, we find gods of maturity, of Autumn, fruitfulness, giving, generosity, plenty. The Element is Water, and the gods of transit, the ferrymen, the subtle changers and gentle teachers are found here. The potent water gods of the ancestral world are here, both as deities of the rivers, oceans, and as local guardians of springs and wells. The cosmic tides of space and time are the higher octave of this Quarter, and so we also find gods of universal love and compassion, the transformative and enabling powers of the spirit in the ocean of Being. The implement of the West is the Cup. The Inner Temple of the West is one of Donation and Reception.

North

In the North, we first find gods of age, of Winter, of death. The Element is Earth; the elder gods are not weak or negative, but filled with the immemorial strength of the Earth, of rock. The higher octaves of this Quarter are those of wisdom, of readiness, and calm. It leads to the comprehension of the night sky and stars. Paradoxically the Earth gods are also the star gods. Here also are the gods of sleep, peace, rest, forgetting, and the final transition from one world to another. Ancestral teachers and guides are found in the North, the gods that communicate wisdom and offer it to us as practical guidance. The implement of the North is the Shield or Mirror. Here is the Dark Mother of the depths of time and space, who draws all unto herself in order that all may be renewed. The Inner Temple of the North is one of Destruction and Regeneration.

In mythic cycles, we often find that a hero or god travels around the Wheel, changing with the seasons. At Spring, he is newly born, filled with the rush and inspiration of life. At Summer, he becomes an adult, holding his peak of power on balance and harmony. By Autumn, he has become the mature man, the giver. At Winter, he is old and wise, often becoming a mentor or teacher. At the transition between North and East, he dies, to be reborn again upon a further turning of the Wheel.

Above

The realm of the sky and stars, revealing the eternal depths within the universe. There is a paradoxical relationship between Above and Below, which is adequately highlighted by modern theories of relativity. In a general sense, the Direction Above is that of Ultimate Divinity—this may be the Sky Father in a simple world model, or it may be Universal Being. Meditations on Above/Below are relative: due to gravity, we think of the sky and stars as "above," when in truth we are within the sphere of which our Solar system is the center, and the stars are equally beyond the horizons of the Four Directions, Above and Below. The Lunar/Earth Sphere or Realm is within the Solar Realm, and both are within the Stellar Realm. Three nested spheres of relative location in the Cosmos.

Below

This is the realm of the Underworld, which paradoxically holds the stars. The Direction Below is that of the Earth Mother, or more universally of the Great Mother of all Being. Above and below can be inverted or reverted at any time, and some very powerful magical techniques consist of exactly this process.

Within

Within is the living spirit, the core or seed of Being. This may manifest to the imagination in innumerable ways: for men it is often the primal Male Child of Light, eternal, unchanging, radiant. For women it may be the Daughter of Light. At its deepest level, the Direction Within touches upon the Source, the utterance of Being out of silence. All Directions, Gods, Goddesses, stars, planets and zones are within, but to merely state this in words is insufficient, a set of phrases that can lead us away from proper contemplation or experience.

CHAPTER 7

The King within

Kingship is associated with the heart or heart center of consciousness and energy. This is the point of poise that harmonizes all energies. The King mediates between the Land (the worker, body or feet) and the Stars (priest, spirit, or head). The King may also partake of all or any Branch; Divine or Sacred Kings were, in theory, if not always in practice, individuals with a fully developed conscious fusion between the Branches of Priest and King. Whatever such Kings enacted for the land and the people was directly inspired or attuned by spiritual power. We are inevitably aware that this Sacred Kingship became a source of hereditary political power that remained in place for thousands of years in various forms, until the early 20th century. Remnants are still found today in many parts of the world. Yet this is not the Sacred Kingship, but the secular Kingship.

In personal terms the Sacred King or central balancing potential brings the potentially conflicting energies and motives of our inner Warrior, Poet, Priest, and Prophet into a proper relationship to one another. Very often this has to be worked through by encountering each Branch until they are balanced with one another. Kingship tends to come after years of developing skills and inner energies through emphasis on other

Branches. Very often, Kingship is found by working upon one's weakest Branch, rather than constantly building upon innate abilities confined within one specific Branch. Spiritual training, even self-training, is no different to physical training. It benefits from discipline, patience, and rhythmic repetition.

The Sacred Kingship

> Voluntary incarnation is the first sacrifice,
> The sacrificial life is the second,
> The sacrificial death is the third.

The Male Mysteries cannot be discussed, approached or brought alive for the future without some preliminary understanding of the major Branch of the Sacred Kingship. It is only through intense practice within the Mystery that we come to a deeper comprehension. There is no claim here, in this book, or by the author, to completely understand or to represent this Branch of the Mysteries in full, or in any so-called "authoritative" manner.

The Sacred Kingship opens out many levels of understanding, many realms of awareness, and no particular individual or school can truthfully lay claim to it. Those that do so, be they single teachers, orders, cults, or world religions, are either deluded or intentionally deceptive. Delusion and illusion are unavoidable conditions of our collective humanity, but they are not irredeemable. Intentional lies regarding spiritual or liberating truths are powerful vehicles of manifest evil and corruption. No single spiritual path to truth and liberation has been so lavishly convolutedly and persistently enmeshed in lies as that of the Sacred Kingship.

Before we begin to examine the Sacred Kingship, be aware that not all men enter this Branch of the Male Mysteries, and that there is no requirement that any individual should do so. Nevertheless, any male wishing to develop through the esoteric traditions and the Five Branches must have some understanding of the Sacred Kingship, as membership of this Mystery may be offered at any time, often under the most surprising or unexpected circumstances. Furthermore, the work of all the other Branches is connected in a harmonic fashion to that of the Sacred Kingship, just as each Branch is interconnected harmonically with the others.

The Sacred Kingship, however, is the deepest or central Branch of the Male Mysteries in our human world. Many aspects of esoteric training, development, and the enablement and transfer of inner energies and spiritual powers, centralize and focus within and from the Sacred Kingship. This Solar core of awareness, likened to the Sun, our Star, has both centrifugal and centripetal powers. It may radiate spiritual transformation and harmony outward, or it may draw us into its deepest heart.

Much has been written on the subject, ranging from anthropological studies of human sacrifice through to refined theology in an orthodox and carefully controlled context.

There is a wide rift between a historical viewpoint of the Sacred Kingship in various primal cultures and early civilizations, and the inner condition or Mystery as a living power. This rift is due to the long-term effect of orthodox religion, which strives to subsume or destroy all Branches of the Mysteries, and to erase all other cults and religions that may be actual or potential rivals.

Within the esoteric traditions, we learn that early, or what we might truthfully call primal, Christianity, before the cult was corrupted by political aims and lust for world domination, was based upon the ancient and widespread Mystery of the Sacrificial and Sacred Kingship. To this extent it was, on the surface, little different from a number of other sacrificial cults that seed, rise, and decay, within the overall ground of human religion through the ages. At the time of its inception, there were many sacrificial cults of death and resurrection in the Mediterranean region, and taking the role of male sacrifice was a relatively normal Mystery path. Despite lurid fiction and films, human sacrifice embodied only the most remote early phases of the Sacred Kingship. Today the sacrifice is within ourselves, though modern heroes may indeed be willing to sacrifice their lives for others.

There is, however, a wealth of spiritual and magical lore concerning the degree or octave of spiritual potential afforded by the sacrifice of Jesus of Nazareth, and his relationship to the consciousness of the solar system, the universe, and ultimate Being.

We may set aside discussion as to the possible truth or falsehood of such esoteric lore; this endless type of argument leads us nowhere other than into the hands of manipulators of dogma and suppression. The degree of truth and falsehood in any inner, transpersonal, fundamental matter of consciousness and entity is always relative. Truth is found through experience rather than theory or dogma. Most of the rival cults, including those more primal forms of Christianity itself, rooted into the perennial religions and wisdom traditions of our world, were forced underground by ruthless persecution of variant sects during the early days of developing politicized Christianity after its adoption as a state religion by the late Roman Empire in 380 CE. The esoteric teachings, however, still exist undamaged, and may be regained or regenerated by certain techniques of altered consciousness.

The underground traditions tended to preserve such techniques and perpetuate them, rather than preserve detailed sets of beliefs, rules, instructions, or information itself. Information without perception or understanding is, needless to say, of no value whatsoever. As time passed and historical or material oppression increased from state religion, it became less and less viable to preserve rigidly detailed sets of alternative beliefs. Much lore was preserved in the dream-like state of the collective imagination, and in folk tradition, rooted into national or tribal and environmental forms.

The esoteric techniques, however, were handed down through personal instruction, or through regeneration within traditional forms. More simply, the techniques cause the inner truths and teachings to regenerate within the individual imagination. There was, therefore, no need to preserve dogma or rigid sets of so-called facts, especially as these were the tools of suppressive state religion. In our present context we need to be aware; first, that true or inner Christianity is a quite different matter from the aggressive male-stereotypical political religion of outer history that we have considered in our earlier chapters. Inner, primal, or esoteric Christianity is based firmly within the ancient Mystery of the Great Goddess and the Sacred Kingship. It can form a core part of the Male Mysteries either as primal Christianity, or as a purely pagan pre-Christian stream, or as a compassionate moral impetus with no religion whatsoever.

An older precedent within the orthodox Judeo-Christian texts, predating that of the sacrifice of Jesus, is that of Melchizedek, an Old Testament figure deriving from the ancient (Pagan) Sacred Kingship practices of the Middle East. One of the most powerful streams of consciousness in the Male Mysteries is known as the Order of Melchizedek, with various expressions ranging from highly orthodox to underground and long-secret fusions of pagan Gnostic and primal Christian tradition, teaching, and esoteric arts and sciences.

The prevailing use of the Old Testament/Torah example, that of Melchizedek, King of Salem, does not limit, and never has limited, the consciousness and energy of the Mystery to a Judeo-Christian context. We shall explore this complex but not insoluble paradox shortly.

The Sacred Kingship is a holism, an inter-resonating pattern of energy and consciousness, enfolding and generating various entities ranging from human to transhuman to divine. Such entities live within one another; they have a constant interaction upon one another; the interaction is timeless, and defies the accepted or habitual barriers of space, physical entity, and energy. Did we but know it, we are all within such states or entities of holism or interaction, male and female. Such is the nature of our environment, our planet, our universe. There are holisms within holisms, and the thresholds between such collectives are thresholds of energy: for humans and other self-conscious entities, these thresholds mark changes of awareness.

Many of the more subtle levels of interaction are only consciously imbued and fully enabled through radical changes of awareness, resonating through changes of the flow patterns or cycles of our vital energies. Through such changes or realignments, time, space, and habitual energy patterns are altered, inverted, even altogether obviated and disposed of. In the magical and spiritual arts and disciplines, such changes are generated through work within specific training programs. Such programs involve the fusion of physical, mental, and imaginative techniques with concepts and images.

One of the results or transformations sought is that of relationships formed with spiritual or inner-world beings. These beings are the spirits, gods, goddesses, and other such entities of religion, myth, and esoteric tradition. The entire subject of divine beings, and the literal or symbolic nature of gods and goddesses is discussed elsewhere in this book.

When we examine the Sacred Kingship, we have a historical picture, well known from many early cultures, involving literal Kingship and literal sacrifice, making a cycle of connections between the human and transhuman or divine worlds and dimensions. But in a modern context this background is merely representative of the manifestation of the Mystery upon a collective level in human life. The Kingship, its sacred quality, and the acts of sacrifice are ultimately inner personal and transpersonal events. Such events work in a different manner for males than for females. Men and women each play equal roles in the Mysteries, and these roles differ from the dreary stereotypes of masculinity and femininity that still permeate our culture today as a result of mass conditioning and suppression. There is no suggestion here that the spiritual sacrificial volunteers are inevitably men, for this is not the case. There is, however, an extensive tradition of men being sacrificed or sacrificing themselves, which seems to have its roots in very early matriarchal and goddess-worshipping cultures. The predominance of men as Sacred Kings, as spiritual sacrifices, or in similar roles, is not, and never has been, any part of the stereotype of male superiority.

Modern genetics seems to mirror, upon a microcosmic, microscopic level, the same pattern that is found in the Mystery—the male unit is, somehow, disposable after he has performed certain functions within the collective being. But that is only part of the picture, for if we limit it to a material biological level, then it is a most unbalanced pattern indeed. The sacrificed or disposable male entity, be it a cell, a sperm, a genetic fragment, or a human, is reborn again and again. Thus the life of the sacrificed male is not a line that terminates, but a spiral, or even a spiral of spirals.

In the context of the Male Mysteries, therefore, we need to discover and to understand why men are sacrificed, and why women traditionally mediate certain functions and aspects of the sacrifice. This spiritual and magical teaching is, fortunately, fully defined in the perennial traditions, though in a number of variant presentations. Such living understanding only comes from experience on a number of levels of consciousness, and not from simply learning lists of attributes or the details of an illustration.

We also need to be endlessly vigilant, to guard against confusing the transpersonal truths of the Mysteries with simple therapeutic processes. There are many levels of consciousness to the Sacred Kingship which are unknown to psychotherapy. We may stay with this important difference for the present, and consider briefly one of the great initiatory changes of consciousness found in esoteric disciplines and training, and its very unique manifestation through the Mystery of the Sacred Kingship.

In all magical traditions worldwide, there is a level of awareness concerning ancestral contact. This may be systematized through modern genetics, or through the Jungian concept of the collective unconscious, but no matter what terminology we use, direct communication with the ancestors is a reality of esoteric initiation. The major difference between this type of connection in the esoteric traditions and in modern genetics or psychology is that the initiate experiences the awareness consciously, and not through a scientific or intellectual model or in any other interface designed in a theoretical manner.

In the Mystery of the Sacred Kingship, this shared consciousness and diffusion of collective experience through time and space is, contrary to the usual manner of collective traditions and consciousness, not genetically dependent. Initiation into the Mystery gives the individual a conscious sharing, a direct contact with the memories and transpersonal modes of awareness of those who have gone before within the Mystery. The many individuals concerned need not be related genetically, and need not have any line of ancestral connectivity.

This potential is found in the source text from Judaic/Semitic tradition, as to the nature of the initiator of Abraham, named Melchizedek, who was "without father or mother." It may also be referred to in the obscure sayings attributed to Jesus of Nazareth concerning the separation of spiritual enlightenment from family ties.

PART III

VISUALIZATIONS AND EXERCISES

CHAPTER 8

Visualizing transformation

The exercises in this book are modern developments, unique to the author, but they are broadly based upon the perennial traditions, techniques, and teachings of the Western Mysteries. With this foundation they derive from a coherent and enduring tradition of ritual transformation, said to have been preserved and actively taught in the West for thousands of years. The traditional techniques for transformation and empowerment may take a variety of forms, and work through several different schools or lineages of contact.

In this book we are dealing specifically with a restatement of the Male Mysteries, so material relating to men is given a special emphasis. The Mysteries, however, are for men and women equally, and the Male and Female Mysteries ultimately unite together. There are times and places where men and women need to work separately, and times and places where they need to work together. The Western Esoteric Tradition, being a universal source of spiritual growth, provides ample working material for all such situations, phases or levels of consciousness.

There is no need, however, for the individual man or group wishing to use the new exercises offered here to become deeply absorbed in the entire vast and complex Western Esoteric Tradition, or to study it in depth. The basic exercises can be attempted straight away with no background study or preliminary work. Indeed, they often work more effectively if no preconception or intellectual study has been established beforehand.

When these exercises are taken at face value, and honestly attempted, they inevitably produce results. They are designed to work on their own, relating to one another through the patterns of relationship described in our various chapters and shown in our illustrations. Some basic skill at visualizing and meditation will be very helpful when you begin the work, but if you have no previous experience in these disciplines, do not be put off. They will work anyway, but the less experienced visualizer or meditator may only become aware of their effect slowly; in some cases, where there are severe blocks upon the imagination, a calm repeated effort is necessary to free up the inner faculties.

Occasionally freedom will come through a cathartic explosive reaction, which unblocks the individual suddenly, establishing a clear perception and sense of returning to a reality and level of consciousness that had almost been lost. This last experience is a common one, particularly for men who have lived for years on false values of assertiveness and merit, having lost touch with their inner nature as a result. These exercises can give considerable help in rebalancing us when we are in the rigid unnatural states still required, even demanded, of men in Western or Westernized cultures.

One of the open secrets of esoteric or spiritual methods of self-transformation is that they are very simple. Everyone assumes that something powerful must be complex or even laborious; this is untrue. Any of the basic visionary exercises in this book may be taken at face value, as a simple event involving images, framed within basic narrative or story-telling, followed by a period of stillness in private. If they are worked in this manner they will produce results that prove clear, powerful, and often surprising.

For many centuries, the hidden traditions required extensive training to take place, and that no student should work with powerful visions, telesms, or god- and goddess-forms until they had undergone a basic course in various supportive disciplines. This requirement is not, as is often assumed, based upon secrecy or elitism, but upon common sense. It is designed to protect the student from accidents, and to build his or her abilities gradually. It still holds good in many of the techniques of ritual magic, advanced visualization, and related arts and disciplines.

But the baseline, or threshold of initiation, has altered somewhat during the 20th century.

During the last few decades, there has been a gradual raising of consciousness and a slow but definite change in the collective imagination in the West. No one should pretend that this is a widespread dawning of mass illumination, but it is clear that people are beginning to pay more attention to inner arts and disciplines. Partly as a result of the increased number of meditators, visualizers, and partly as a result of deep changes of collective consciousness which have occurred, it is possible to offer attuned and powerful exercises for almost immediate use.

Visualization, exercises, and energies

Three distinct paths or broadly defined methods of working with inner energies can be easily distinguished. As a general rule, we tend to combine these in varying ways, though they can each be exclusively developed as specific systems of training. Examples of each are found throughout the world.

The first is physical use of the body. Movement, posture, and polarity working (such as sexual activity) can arouse and transform energies. Techniques such as yoga, tai-chi, warrior skills and arts, dance, and ritual movement or polarity work of any physical sort, are all examples of this path.

The second is through personal meditation and concentration. In such techniques, the meditator focuses upon the inner energies and brings them through consciously, whereas they had previously been dormant or automatic and unconscious. This path includes many techniques of conscious or willed arousal of our individual power-centers (often loosely termed chakras), and those vast traditions of spiritual and mystical meditation and contemplation in which the individual passes within to increasingly deeper levels of being, until the inner power or divinity is met. The life-power or divinity is, in the latter stages of such work, consciously brought out to transform the entire entity, and then to flow or radiate to the outer world.

The third path is that of imagery, visualization, and the use of god- and goddess-forms. This is the way of the magical primal mythic or ancient religious traditions, and is probably the least understood and least practiced today. Upon this path, the individual or group does not necessarily focus upon inner energies directly, but encounters living images or inner-world beings. These are usually defined through a mythic structure as gods, goddesses, or as transcendent or Underworld beings, often closely linked to the land or to Elemental forces in nature.

The encounter and exchange of energies within such visualizations and meetings has a distinct effect upon the individual, and will act very deeply indeed in some cases. Thereafter he or she may be able to draw consciously upon energies that were previously blocked or dormant. Many primal magical and sophisticated magical arts depend upon such interactions. There is a vast store of half-obscured knowledge concerning the procedures, and individual traditions rely upon meetings with specific beings, such as ancestors, spiritual animals, gods and goddesses, and inner-world teachers. In specific traditions, the same entities may persist for thousands of years virtually unchanged, or may manifest through variant forms according to cultural changes. The simplest way of defining this path is to regard it as a highly amplified and accelerated variant of the life cycle, and of our usual growth through encounters with other people and ensuing transformational experiences.

It is for this reason that such techniques frequently use the Wheel of Life (Figure 1), which shows the resonance and holism between the Four Elements, the Four Seasons, the Directions, and the human life cycle. Specific transformative and initiatory or teaching entities are located in different Quarters of the Circle, and we progress around it or toward them by highly energized means in vision and ritual pattern making. This type of work was central to the ancient Mysteries, and can be startlingly effective in modern use.

Envisioning the future

Meditation has received considerable popular attention in the last 40 years, though there are a number of quite different interpretations of what, exactly, meditation is and what the meditator's aims and methods, if any, should be. Such interpretations range from those embedded within religious or spiritual traditions, such as yogic, Hindu, Buddhist, Sufi, or Christian meditation, all being effective methods yet quite distinct from one another, to general techniques of many varieties. Such general techniques, widely found in the New Age movement, vary considerably; some of the popular types would not strictly seem to be meditation at all but consciously induced daydream or reverie. Perennial and esoteric or magical arts employ very precise techniques of meditation, usually embedded within little-known traditions and schools of inner development.

Visionary practice has, until recently, been given less popular prominence, but is now used in various schools of general meditation, therapy, and for a range of what would traditionally be considered spurious reasons such as "getting what you want." This commercial aspect of using visualization to obtain desired ends, is now widely sold in popular books and recordings. It is a typical example of our modern fragmentary techniques of accessing or altering consciousness, too often used in superficial or potentially damaging contexts.

Yes, we can get what we want through visualization; this simple fact has been known for millenniums, but there is a risk of such wanting backfiring on us. A simple but profound teaching from the Western tradition has been restated by several proponents as: "Be careful in what you ask for, as you might get it." How many times have we all regretted asking for something in everyday life, wishing for something, or someone, to happen to us, and then, after our wish has been granted, saying "If only I'd known ..." To seek apparent benefit from our wishes, we should first know what we really want.

Knowing what we want should, then, be related to what we truly need, and at some point after this, we may indeed gain some insight into a balanced target for certain types of wish-fulfilling visualization.

The esoteric traditions use our inherent ability to envision in a quite different way, usually in the context of a mythic or collective framework, and in practice tied into very specific images or holisms of imagery and energy. The perennial wisdom traditions worldwide have always taught this: whatever we want transforms us until we want it no longer. This truth is employed in magical ritual, and in meditation and visualization, using images and what seem to be defined goals and ends purely for the transformative effect that they have. When these transformative acts are undertaken, we usually cannot know in full what effect they might have—they are often leaps in the dark. Traditional teachings, however, when sensibly assessed, provide certain general but significant guidelines as to how the techniques work, and where they often (but not inevitably) lead.

No man who longs and strives to become a Master can ever succeed in his wish. If he does achieve liberation he finds that the mastery which he sought is now behind him or, as is more commonly experienced, that it is ever beyond him—it is a means and not an end.

The conflict between what we think we want, what we have been forced or conditioned to want, and what the deeper often masked or blocked resonances of ourselves may want, can be devastating. Sometimes not one of these apparent wants, at any accessible level, will be harmonious to our deepest or spiritual needs; a moment inevitably comes when the spiritual impetus directs or seeks a course totally counter to the conditions or habits of life. Such deep utterances of our essential being cannot be addressed or resolved by mental therapy, but must be experienced in full, even if they lead to terrible and outwardly irresolvable situations. Fortunately for most of us a high degree of spiritual impetus or volition is rare. We usually receive it second hand, so to speak, from the resonance of the lives of great spiritual mediators, teachers, saints, heroes, and heroines. Such people, male and female, are not limited to the world's roll-call of prominent historical or cult characters with claims to spiritual status—many are anonymous, some are reviled, yet their impetus remains.

The problem of relating want and need is often bitterly experienced by modern men, who are, even when aware of the problem, in despite of themselves, conditioned to achieving goals, making grades, gaining obvious and accredited or rewards merits, essentially confusing greed with need. Many men, of course, are not aware of any problem, only of a dimly felt but unresolved inner conflict and tension, which is increased rather than alleviated by gaining, striving, and apparently succeeding. The modern phenomenon of stress, manifesting widely in men, but found in both men and women, is one obvious yet frustratingly elusive and insoluble illness deriving from inner conflict with outer situations and circumstances. A man is not stressed by pressure in the workplace so much as by pressure to engage in pointless work, to deliver results that benefit remote wealth, though not his own. Only an elite few receive the benefits of work done mostly by others.

The individual male is often under a heavy pressure to seek so-called security in outer forms such as status, possessions, appearance, popularity, and so forth. This also applies to development of skills, egocentric competitiveness, sexual gratification, and fame. Very few people, men or women, turn-about and ask where, exactly, does this pressure come from? Only when we begin to ask questions does it begin to fade, for it is an illusion that perpetuates itself only through acceptance; it consists of energy misaligned and misplaced. Western society was literally imagined or imaged into its present state of vicious imbalance and self-destruction. It only needed greed to follow, and of course we are often greedy.

The "discovery" of visualization

In (approximately) the 1950s, visualization was "discovered" through an unfortunate fusion of an assorted ragbag of consciousness-transforming techniques and popular psychotherapy. It was loudly hailed as a guaranteed means of gaining nebulous materialist ends such as wealth and indomitable willpower. For the last half-century and more it has been given numerous purchasable presentations, ranging from cheap paperback books to very expensive courses presented to clients in exclusive retreat or shipboard surroundings.

Visualization has also been used widely in alternative therapies. Certain techniques involving color, gentles scenarios or dream-like locations, often linked to specific music, are essentially loose fragments from the perennial spiritual and esoteric traditions of altering consciousness. Some popular modern therapeutic techniques can be traced directly or by implication to spiritualism and Theosophical Society origins in the 19th century, even though they are now used in a purely materialist context such as psychotherapy or alternative treatment for stress or incurable disease.

Strictly speaking, the best cure for many of the imbalances treated by such alternative methods is to cure the vicious society and the inner and outer pollution that causes such illnesses, rather than concentrate, however compassionately, effectively or validly, upon individual manifestations. But this global cure would, of course, be too idealist and unprofitable.

Before we proceed with visualizations relevant to the Male Mysteries, it is worth reassessing the function and effect of envisioning. Even if you are familiar with or experienced in focused envisioning, this short reassessment may be valuable in the context of the specific visualizations in this book.

Why visualize?

Why should we visualize? First, we need to be aware that conscious visualization, as a specific exercise, is a special development of a mode of awareness that we experience ceaselessly. The imagination, our image-making capacity of consciousness, works continuously, though often upon a subliminal level, below a threshold that we seldom consciously cross. Visualization involves steering the imagination through conscious adaptation and controlled generation of chosen sets of images: but it does not remain at that initial level, as anyone working with the exercises in this book will discover.

Our imagination today is focused and consciously engaged through media broadcast on our smartphones, through reading, music, drama, radio, and to a lesser extent film, and to an even lesser extent through television. As a general rule, the more obviously detailed and specific a series of externalized images is, such as television, and entertainment on our ubiquitous smart phones where visual images are externalized upon a very small surface, the less stimulus they provide for the imagination. No comment or general criticism is being passed here on relative merits or quality as this is an altogether different discussion, merely upon the simple effects of certain media upon the imagination, regardless of the content of the material that they convey.

With the enormous surge of social media and smart phones, we enter a stage of mass addiction to stimuli that isolate us from the outer world, yet restrict us from individually expanding our imagination. The addictive aspects of social media have been discussed in a number of recent books, and have become a major concern as a means of disseminating propaganda and bizarre theories that become massively inflated with no real foundation.

In our context of the Male Mysteries, such addictions are driven not only by content, but by the emissions or energy fields of our computers and smartphones. These are known to have a deleterious effect upon the body, which we just ignore and continue to absorb.

Most of all, the imagination is stunted, as it becomes increasingly dependent on exterior stimulus from small sources that lock the attention and the body into a rigid conformity ... shared by millions, built to capture, and all for control and profit. Thus do we isolate ourselves from nature, from life, while assuming that we are in the company of many friends.

The imagination atrophies if it is not used. Widespread visual technology has resulted in a substantial lowering of our individual and collective image-making abilities. Curiously, when the imagination atrophies, so does the memory, the length of attention-span, and many other aspects of consciousness. It is as if the holism of human consciousness is energized by the imagination. We shall return to this possibility shortly.

Concentrated image-making as a deliberate controlled activity is, even without the degenerative effect of our modem toys and entertainments, very rare. We are perhaps more familiar today with random image-making in the association processes that are highlighted and used in therapy. Free association and similar random association methods were, and are, not used in the esoteric traditions. Under some circumstances, such as heightened consciousness or in highly energized groups or powerful geomantic sites and sacred locations, free association and random drifting can be detrimental to the individual—the inner equivalent of wandering idly across a busy freeway.

Ancient visions: modern applications

To understand where the magical or perennial spiritual traditions of envisioning come from, we can consider collective myth-making and poetry or storytelling. This is where the imagination is discovered to be the energizing source for other expressions or modes of awareness; the memory, the power of attention and concentration, and the higher consciousness of empathy, compassion and spiritual liberation.

Historically we find that mythic lore was embodied in long poems and tales. Some of the great mythic epics took not hours but days to tell; furthermore, people truly listened to them, retold them, and held them within their minds and imaginations as an integral part of their lives. Such concepts seem almost impossible to us today, yet they are still present in potential in every human being. Furthermore, primal peoples in isolated regions today sing long epic ballads, tell long tales, and consciously relate such mythic material to the creation of their land, their ancestors, and on initiatory levels, to magical and spiritual transformation and empowerment. It is these levels of imagination that need to be restored and employed in any modern equivalent or restatement of the Mysteries, be it for men, women, individuals, or groups. Anything less is merely an intellectual exercise or a fabrication with no living source.

There is little point in expecting modern men and women to learn epic tales, dances, and dramas relating to the creation of the world or of the Cosmos. In any case, we do not live according to the social patterns in which such mythic lore was created and preserved. But we still have the core elements, the foundation, of this lore within us, for creation myth and certain key images are both preserved and regenerated at the deepest levels of our consciousness, our entity, our being. The old magical and spiritual traditions encapsulated their collective diffuse mythic lore into concise sets of images, into god- and goddess-forms, and into certain key patterns and tales, used both in visualization and in ritual dance or ceremonial magic.

If we seek to transform ourselves, our imagination is the most potent tool to use. Once the imaging faculty has been awakened, and this is surprisingly easy for most of us, it draws to itself and empowers many other aspects of consciousness and energy. The imagination is very closely linked to our sexual energies; we might say that they are polarized manifestations of the same life and death forces that reside within us all.

The more advanced techniques in traditional magical arts or spiritual meditation and envisioning always involve our sexual energies, though not necessarily in any physically gratifying activity. The sexual energies, called the Inner Fire in the Western traditions, are aroused by imagination, but the imagery need not be, and in practice seldom is, sexual as modem people understand sexuality. The popular delusions, frequently published, of magical arts involving orgies, non-consensual sex, or unusual physical sexual acts are simply generated by wishful thinking, but they are also perpetuated and inflamed by commercial and religious vested interests. This region of fantasy (as distinct from deeper imagination) can become addictive and compulsive.

It is interesting to note that the most repellent and unnatural acts are often voiced (when accusing other religions, pagans, magicians, and so forth) by people in fundamental religious movements. They seem to need to accuse others of whatever they themselves hide in their most secret fantasies. Or perhaps this is too harsh a judgement, and they are merely so insecure in their own beliefs that they need to find negative images of other peoples' ways and worship to reassure themselves in moments of doubt and despair. Compassion seems to have no place in such nightmares, so, inevitably, the regenerative purifying energy of the imagination is seldom allowed to unfold and flower.

Strength and Falling Towers

Thus imagination and visualization may be used for positive liberating ends, or for negative suppressive ends. Ironically, most people male and female, use their inherent divine power of imaging to imprison themselves, even to degrade themselves. Once the imagination and sexual energies become linked in a cycle or loop of negative implication and effect, it requires special effort to suspend such patterns and break away from them. Special effort need not imply strenuous effort, or prolonged therapy. Many of the visions found in the Mysteries will undertake this task for us—not necessarily as a prime effect, but merely through their inevitable realignment of our innermost energies.

Often in matters of consciousness and energy, if we set out to envision or meditate with a specific end in mind, we defeat that end, or reinforce its opposite tendency within ourselves. Traditional methods, however, involve imagery and energies, often associated with ancient divine entities, that empower but initially break down our conditioned inner constructs, patterns, habits, and addictions.

Such constructs exist upon at least two levels; the collective or human holism, and the individual level, which accumulates in one lifetime. In the esoteric traditions, we learn that there are also resonances and patterns of energy carried over from what appear to be previous lives. This is, perhaps, the simplest way of stating the greatly misrepresented and misunderstood laws of reincarnation and the popular idea of karma.

The breaking-down of patterns is, in itself, not too difficult to achieve. There is an increasing move toward implementing such psychic breakdown in alternative therapies and group work loosely based upon primal traditions; but because the cathartic or catabolic breaking-down is easy to induce, and because the balancing, anabolic or building training and imagery take years for a conscientious teacher or guide to acquire and use effectively, there can be problems. Once again we find that problems arise because cathartic techniques are nowadays taken out of their proper life context and spiritual or transformative tradition, and used diffusely in the therapeutic or experiential modern group. Such borrowing is often not, in itself, enough to fully regenerate or liberate us.

The imagination is one of the more obviously definable manifestations of our well-spring of life and energy; this is exactly why the imagination and the sexual energies are so closely intertwined. If we are truly able to envision, we can change not only ourselves, but the form and manifestation of the world around us. This concept is at the foundation of ritual magic; the word magic is a close relative of the word imagination—imaging in or out from the Source of Being.

When confronted with this proposition, most people assume that it takes truly titanic amounts of effort, energy, willpower, and discipline to re-route their habits of imagination. This would be true, if we were to attempt to serially and literally recondition all that has arisen and patterned itself within us during our entire lives to the present moment. But the massive application of willpower and effort are frequently counter-productive; they are often associated with the overkill that is typical to the male delusion of riding roughshod over problems, cutting through knots, heaving boulders from the path, and so forth. This delusion is by not confined exclusively to men, though it is often stated to be a typically male attitude. At present it is deeply rooted in the habits and language of our culture, thus it affects both men and women, particularly those in a position of power. The scale of such power ranges from personal relationships to world economics and politics.

We are not so much individuals upon blocked paths, but the very paths and boulders themselves. We have to roll ourselves away to be reborn, rather than think that some technique, Master, bought-in salvation, or exclusive religion will do it for us.

Curiously we find this truth stated in the most modern of sciences, that of computer prediction through complex mathematical models. In recent years scientists have theorized and modeled results that even in the most rigorous mathematical models, the beating of a bird's wing in an isolated forest can and does affect our global weather.

That which is powerful, as the mystical traditions have always taught, is that which is very slight, imperceptible, and yet which permeates all. If Alexander the Great had known exactly where and when to sneeze, rather than draw his sharp bright sword, the Gordian Knot would have unraveled completely—even if our hero had been thousands of miles distant from it.

In Tarot, two Triumphs (major cards) reveal this truth: the Blasted Tower and Strength. Both emblems also feature in mythic or spiritual traditions that predate the appearance of Tarot cards,[24] and have their counterparts in the legends and literature of world religion. The Blasted Tower is a construct unnaturally held together and upright by force, long after it should have reached a state of collapse and decay leading to regeneration. This image is usually one of a show of power and despotic will being blasted and destroyed by natural (i.e., divine) forces. The polar opposite or partner is Strength, in which a savage primal beast, usually a lion, is shown under the imperceptible yet certain control of a gentle maiden. In some modern Tarot decks this has been altered into a male strongman such as Hercules wrestling the beast down, but to do so isolates the image from its deep roots and true meaning. When such emblems are understood in pairs, or more subtly, in triads and quaternaries, they begin to fully work for us.

Visualization realigns our energies; they are carried along with and through the pattern or story of the intentional vision; we emerge beyond it transformed, regenerated, and empowered. Yet, because we are transformed, many of our notions of so-called power are lost en-route. It is quite likely that if we are to seek spiritual Masters and men of power in the outer world, that they exist in the most obvious and unnoticed places. They are certainly not supermen living in special communities or in isolated parts of the planet. A Master, assuming he existed at all, would consider such self-indulgence to be weakness indeed. Why be superhuman when you could, instead, be free?

The true spiritual traditions go even further, and say why be free when your fellow humans are still enslaved? There can be no elite or elect in a whole world, in a pleroma or a fully aware universe.

Envisioning: the basic methods of visualizing

1. A period of calm, of stillness, and simple meditation is first undertaken to clarify consciousness. This may be unified with rhythmic breathing, and should be done with eyes closed. Do not use complex prayers, chants, mantras and so forth, even if you are used to working with these. The aim is to simply be still and prepare the imagination for the intentional vision which is to follow. (Appendix 1 is a modern version of a traditional ancient method for approaching Silence.)
2. A chosen narrative and sequence of images is then built in your imagination, either through someone reading or reciting the imagery aloud (if you are working in a group), or from a recorded source if you are working alone. This last method is a productive way of using modern technology for inner development. As is often argued, the technology itself need not be imprisoning or enervating; it is the way we use it, or succumb to its allure, that causes problems.

Another well-proven method is to read the visualization aloud to yourself several times, until you begin to know it well. Then begin to work with it in silence with eyes closed. You will find that far from being a laborious test of memory, the images begin to come through easily. It is quite acceptable to work with eyes closed, but the text open on your lap; if, in the early stages, you falter, simply open your eyes and read the passage aloud to yourself; then return to working with closed eyes, building the images as clearly as possible. You will soon be able to work without the text.

The secret of this technique lies in not attempting to learn each guided vision as a test of memory, but simply to read it aloud to yourself until you are familiar with it. During the readings, you will gradually build the sequence into your imagination; the mind remembers repeated sequences heard and told aloud far more readily than it does material from the printed page.

This deep memory is particularly enhanced when we use magical or archetypical imagery and narratives. Such techniques have been active for thousands of years, and may be traced historically to cultures such as Ancient Greece and Egypt, which used such mythic narratives in religion, in training for priests and priestesses, and in the Mysteries. The historical ambience of a magical or spiritual technique, however, is merely a series of surface connections; on deeper levels far more is discovered by practice and involvement than can ever be researched or described intellectually.

The relative merits of each method

There are quite distinct advantages and possible disadvantages to each of the methods described, and each will produce varying results and potentials within the overall framework of any visualization. Let us consider each method briefly:

1. Pre-recorded audio
    Using recordings gives a regular rhythm and structure to the visualizations; they may be enhanced by special music, which is usually an aid to imaginative work (providing it does not become a distraction or a habitual prop). The disadvantages of audio are most likely to be connected to dependence. We should not become dependent upon a technological aid toward changing consciousness, so we should not fall into the habit of envisioning or meditating solely to a pre-recorded sequence of words or music. Audio will gradually seem too rigid and predefined after repeated use. Some aspects of this

problem may be obviated with a pause switch. Gradually you will be able to work without the recording.

2. Group work with a reader or reciter
   Once again, the structure is defined by the voice of the reader, who steers the sequence for the vision. An experienced visualizer can work while reading a text aloud, and a really good group guide will work entirely from memory. This gives the opportunity to pace and vary the silent periods, or in the case of advanced work, to improvise certain sections of the visualizations.

   The potential disadvantage of this method is that it is often difficult to find a competent and inspiring reader. A mutually supportive group of men will take in turns to read. This helps to ensure that there is no star or leader status building up. In group work for men, there are many undercurrents of striving and seeking after (false) authority, carried over from the consensual outer life. The life that we are attempting to redeem.

   Another difficult area in reading aloud is how to judge and create the improvised sections. There can be a tendency for the reader to wander off into increasingly vague disconnected visions, losing the intended focus. The key a successive envisioning for a group of men (or women) is to stay attuned to the main imagery and not wander away from it. There may indeed be individual forays and departures during the silent stages of a working ... but they should also return. The return is not only for the individual man, but for the group that mutually support and strengthen one another.

   Originally what we today call visualizations were encapsulated in epic poetry, song, and storytelling. In subsequent centuries-old tales and songs that provided fireside entertainment for communities often held deeper levels, available for those who wished to know. Here we return to the Mysteries.

3. Reading aloud to yourself
   Reading aloud can be a slow process initially, but is very effective. The body responds to the voice, the memory responds to the spoken word. Eventually, reading aloud leads to the living memory of the original text, and great freedom of consciousness. If there is a moment of forgetting in the meditation, the source text should always be present to remind us.

CHAPTER 9

Magic gods and visions

Essentially magic is a collection of arts and esoteric sciences reaching far back into ancestral beliefs and practices, but slowly updated and reassessed within each century. It is based simply upon the use of the human imagination and associated vital energies to interact with other energies, entities, and images. It permeates religion, art, music, literature, folklore, and tradition. In the ancient world, magic was the source of sophisticated and powerful techniques of inner transformation and therapy, with a detailed understanding of human psychology in both mythic and metaphysical terms.

It has often been suggested that the science of today was the magic of yesterday, as if the evolution of consciousness was linear: from magic to science by way of religion; magic and religion disposed of = science reigns. Yet this is mere reductionism, of the "ever upward and onward" type. Many forms of magic permeate religion and science, albeit in subtle guises, while continuing to evolve in their own right. It might be somewhat true to say that science has clarified and dissolved many superstitions in the so-called Western world … a world that now embraces much of the planet with its technology.

A great proportion of magic is holistic, concerned with the wholeness and interrelationship of living creatures and the land and planet.

Due to 19th-century intellectual occultism, this major aspect of magical tradition has been minimized until recently; now, it is undergoing a considerable revival of attention. Contemporary concern with interrelationships, holism of life forms, and the environment, has helped to dispose of the rigid notion that all magical arts are essentially superstitious nonsense. No one will deny that there is much ignorance and superstition in the material purporting to be magical, handed down through the centuries. Ignorance and superstition abound in every aspect of human life—though often the superstition manifests as irrational prejudice and bigotry.

Practical magic is not limited to historical inheritance or slavish adherence to tradition. Each generation contributes certain organic changes to the overall structure of any spiritual or magical tradition, without necessarily moving away from or demolishing the tradition itself. This is because the magical arts are founded upon the collective sources of mythology and human consciousness in relationship to the land or planet. Nowadays, we might say that magic is environmental. The changes in techniques and attitudes to magical arts are in part reflections of changes in society—though students of esoteric philosophy might suggest that changes in society are anticipated or even given impetus by changes in the magical arts.[25]

The concerns of magicians of one generation often manifest at large in the society of later generations—sometimes the manifestation is rapid, sometimes it is slow and subtle, permeating through long periods of historical time.

Here we can focus upon the use of images in magical arts, upon the wide range of interrelated techniques in which the imagination is used in a relatively controlled manner, according to traditional patterns and techniques. The aim of this aspect of magic is to define certain key images and interact with them, to exchange and amplify energy through such interaction. This technique comes under the general heading of visualization nowadays, and is widely used in various schools of meditation and therapy. As the magical arts inherit and still work with material from a variety of religious, mythic and cultural sources, we frequently use images of gods and goddesses for visualization in magic.

Many people are familiar with visualization of deities or mythic beings through the development of the theory of archetypes in Jungian, post-Jungian, and transpersonal psychology. This helps, to a certain extent, in presenting magical art to a modern perception. While such a therapeutic approach does indeed play a part in the magical arts, magical techniques, and practices go further. One confused area of understanding for modern individuals, and indeed of practice in contemporary magical arts, is that of the reality or apparent reality of magical images such as goddess- or god-forms. This confusion is the result of emphasis upon materialism and simplistic reason ... if I cannot kick it, it cannot exist.

We frequently find modern magicians talking and even writing that one may use a god-form to embody certain inherent psychic properties or energies, or to clarify one's own thinking through the therapeutic effect of such images. Even the important word archetype (which has an Ancient Greek origin) has been widely misrepresented through the influence of psychology. Men now frequently consider the presence or power of a god, or the God, as a projection of an archetype, as some fragment of the male psyche.

In some modern books on magic, this psychic fragment is said to benefit males by being projected or extruded as an imaginative form, filled with energy by various esoteric methods, and then deflated and reabsorbed. We might be tempted to observe the Freudian phallic undertones to this post-Jungian theory of magic!

Magic is often regarded solely as an art or esoteric science by which such projections are made. In all the magical arts, as in pagan religion, the god- and goddess-forms are living entities, which act as vehicles or holistic aspects or harmonics of a universal God and Goddess, and are never regarded as projections of the human psyche. This might be flippantly considered as evidence of the ignorance of our ancestors, were it not for the fact that there is often a highly developed understanding of the human psyche in ancient religion, magic, metaphysics, and esoteric or magical practices. Indeed, complex and highly sophisticated discussions on this very subject permeated the philosophy and magical arts of the Classical world, and are known from even earlier sources such as Assyrian or Babylonian and Egyptian texts and fragments.

So our first premise is that the god (by which we mean any aspect of male-imaged divinity) in Western magical arts is a real entity. This divine entity takes a number of forms defined by various streams of myth and religion; it is not a matter of faith or belief, but a matter of testing through experience. The god-forms or entities behave in quite distinct and characteristic ways when encountered in meditation, vision, or ritual working. Our second premise is that these god-forms, variations of expression of a universal God (just as goddesses are variations of the Universal Goddess), are not always subsumed under any one orthodox religious heading. Many god-forms or images lead progressively toward a central figure, often defined as the Son of Light, having centralizing, harmonizing solar powers. This god-form and related consciousness is not controlled or owned by any one orthodox religion.

Furthermore, there are streams of consciousness and imagery, aspects of the god, which do not lead to this solar or central god-form. These can be of major importance in the arts of spiritual transformation, and until recently have been given little attention in modern research publications and practice. For centuries the associated techniques were secret, due to the pervasive threat of torture and execution. We might well wonder why these arts, deriving from supposedly superseded ancient tradition, generated such fear and insecurity in the dominant and male-dominated religions.

The question of polarity comes into all discussions and practices of this sort. The Light Son has been related in literature to a Dark Mother. But we seldom encounter any suggestion that we should work with a Dark Son and a Light Mother. This seems to be the result of patriarchal political religion and monosexual propagandized images of divinity. Our ignorance of the absence of the Dark God is a terrible indictment upon our culture, just as much as our knowledge of the absence of the Dark Goddess.

An essential distinction

We need to be very clear at this point. We are not talking about images of evil when we discuss dark god- and goddess-forms. There is a classic problem in this context found among modern meditators, visualizers, and practitioners, one which runs more deeply than personal psychological manifestations or life problems. A typical scenario, rather comical if it were not so serious, is the one in which the would-be magician seeks to invoke the great God of the ancient world, known variously as Pan or Cernunnos (to whom we shall return shortly in more detail). Such invocations are always, without exception, successful, though the effect may vary from hidden and permeating results over a period of time, to a full sense of contact and presence and considerable power.

If anything like the second effect occurs, the poor religiously-conditioned, materialist-ridden magician often feels that he or she has conjured up something difficult, even evil, because of the level of raw power and the nature of the god himself. No sooner is the god present than he is hastily requested to depart! But the evil is in us, not in the god; if we were to pass through the panic and emerge on the other side, we would find that the god cleanses us of our corruptions, and that we no longer reflect our own fears and imbalances into exterior forms, be they humans or deities. As discussed in our earlier chapters, "Masters" have tended to replace the gods and heroes of the ancient world, performing similar functions but with an emphasis upon nondivinity due to historical monotheism. The variety of male images and god-forms in Western magic is large. How much of this variety derives from purely literary sources and how much from practicing magicians and living tradition is difficult to establish in a strictly historical sense. More important is their general presence within an enduring tradition. This presence within the stream or flow of tradition is significant indeed, for it reveals the difference between a genuine god (or goddess) image, however masked or faint, and the product of modern fantasy or entertainment. God-forms do, of course appear in modem fantasy and entertainment, but not all images or characters that are said to be magical are truly so.

Let us examine some of the basic sources for god-forms, always bearing in mind that these are also the basic sources for goddess-images.

The Tree of Life

Most images are definable upon the Tree of Life, a pan-cultural symbol that shows relationships between various traditional orders of existence, such as gods and goddesses, spirits, angels, and so forth, the human psyche and spirit, and the solar system (see Figure 2). The Tree of Life is often described, in various publications, as deriving from Jewish mysticism and Kabbalah, but it has many Western variants, plus, of course, further expressions worldwide.[26]

The form currently in use seems to be a fusion of neo-Platonic tradition with Renaissance Kabbalah and planetary and Classical mythic patterns. It is a combination of Classical Greek, Jewish, Arabic, and Western European lore such as that of bardic wisdom teachings and other poetic systems preserved in Europe for many centuries. Complex as all this sounds or reads on paper the result is surprisingly simple and accessible.

The Tree of Life is a pattern that reappears, in variant forms, in each tradition regardless of cultural or historical origins. It does so because of its inherent properties, by which our consciousness relates, even unwittingly, to the patterns of the solar system and stars through the Three Worlds or Realms of Earth/Moon, Sun/Planets, and Stars/Cosmos.

Regardless of any origin theories, the ubiquitous Tree of Life exists, and performs the remarkable task of linking and harmonizing all inner or mythic patterns with those of the outer world, be it in the form of the human being or the solar system.

Origins and mirroring of God-forms in Western magic

God-forms, by which we can include for the moment telesms of archangels, angels, and spiritual entities, though these are not true god-forms in their own right, come in a surprising number of guises.

If we take an image such as an archangel found in both Jewish and Christian orthodox religions, we find this same entity in mystical practices and ritual magic. While in an orthodox sense, the archangel may be clearly defined, though in modern Christianity virtually defunct and ignored, in the magical arts the deeper resonance of the image often comes through. These deeper levels may contain old god-forms, which the official religion has subsumed. Thus we cannot strictly call archangels, angels, heroes, saints, and so forth god-forms, but in certain circumstances and through alterations of consciousness, we may find god-forms attuned to them or awakening through their initial interface.

In the magical tradition, such forms are derived from Classical, Middle Eastern, Celtic, and, less frequently nowadays, Norse or Scandinavian tradition. The Middle Eastern variants are confined to those of Islamic (Sufi) and Jewish religious origins, or of Christianity, though much of the Christianity in magical arts is inherited from Gnostic sources rather than Eastern or Roman orthodoxy. Archangels, however, play a strong role in Islam and in the Sufi practices of working with angels and jinn.

There are further connections to Ancient Egyptian religion, through the mirroring of god-forms within one another, but the majority of Egyptian symbolism in Western magical arts was assembled no earlier than the 19th century. Exceptions to this are genuine Egyptian magical papyri which appeared in Europe from time to time, but these were of a late period and not necessarily connected to the ancient religion, more to Renaissance magic, Gnosticism, neo-Platonic tradition, and so forth.

The quality of mirroring is important when we consider images and the forces within the images of gods and goddesses in meditation, magic, and spiritual traditions. Although we can use the term mirroring (thinking of the visual aspect of an infinity-box where mirrors are arranged to reflect one another), the concept is also one of holism, for there is no true original of any god-form. We consider an image, usually defined by collective mythic tradition; within that image are older forms, variant forms, and, to the skilled seer, future forms. Like the box of mutually reflecting mirrors, they mirror one another to infinity. For practical purposes we are usually aware of a specific set or a limited number of images, as the greater whole is implicit in the part ... providing we can access an appropriate part.

This is where a practicing magician and an intellectual occultist or theoretician differ considerably. Both work with sets of images and patterns, but the theorist tends to define originals into a rigid set. The working seer or magician knows that images will change repeatedly, revealing inner aspects of themselves, yet always remain harmoniously true to the original starting image. Much confusion arises for students who cannot initially grasp this, and who seek rigid even dogmatic forms, often at the expense of true magical experience. Men are particularly prone to this problem in Western society, and tend to seek rigid authoritarian hierarchical god-forms and structures.

An example of the mirroring of god-forms will help to explain this process. We can begin with the rather mysterious and virtually ignored English Saint George. He is a mythic saint; in other words, he was not a historical martyr. Indeed, the Roman Church removed him from the modern approved list of saints, as such mythic figures are generally set aside in the ongoing process of ossification and collapse within orthodox religions.

Saint George, patron saint of England, is really a magical image: the hero and the dragon, found in Classical myth such as Perseus. He also links to the Archangel Michael, often used as the model of (patriarchal) Light subduing Darkness. But is this sufficient? If we look within these images, particularly that of Saint George, a remarkable sequence unfolds. It leads us away from a patriotic English Saint and dragon-slayer, toward a primal god of light and liberty, who does not kill the dragon or serpent of the Earth, but is in truth empowered and set free by its transformative forces.[27]

The earliest Basilicas and churches of Saint George, in Lydda, Palestine, are built upon ritual temple sites dedicated to Horus, the hawk god of Egypt. Saint George is sometimes shown with a hawk's head—symbol of pure dawn, flight into the eye of the sun. And, suddenly, this leads us westwards again, to an ancient youthful god of Spring in Celtic tradition, *Gwalchmai* the Hawk of May. This is only the merest summary of a series of connections supported by history, iconography, and archaeology. But in both psychological and magical terms, such mirrored gods are greatly empowering, while the rigid, firmly attributed images are always in danger of becoming stereotypes, or, more subtly, of imbuing stereotypes into the individual psyche.

Gods and visions

A second example of a complex god-form, yet harmonically mirrored, is that of Merlin. People are surprised at the proposal that Merlin is a god rather than a magician, but it seems likely that historically the name Merlin or more likely "Myrddin" was a title assumed by certain prophets within a Welsh and Scottish line of tradition. This tradition links back both to the Goddess of the Land from early cultures in the West, and to her divine son or consort. We are fortunate to have records of Irish myth, preserved (ironically) by monastic scribes, and Welsh manuscript sources that likewise tell of mythic powers associated with native deities, gods and goddesses alike.

Today, of course, Merlin is seen as a stereotypical wise elder in modern fiction and popular belief, but we find that the earliest legends of Merlin show an entire life cycle, from prophetic youth to mad wildman of the woods, and only then to the elder. Merlin, particularly the young Merlin, is associated with the polarized power of two dragons within the Earth, Red and White. The earliest Merlin texts, from the 12th century are concerned with prophetic vision, and knowledge of many worlds and orders of creation. The prophecies are uttered by Merlin as a boy, underground as the dragons rise up, reminiscent of the myth of the child Apollo and the serpent at Delphi.[28]

So within the stereotypical elder Merlin is a harmonic set of reflections leading to a divinity, the primal Child of Light. As many of these connectives are shown in the pattern of the Tree of Life, let us now proceed to a summary of god-forms in Western magic, referring to Figure 2.

God-forms upon the Tree of Life

God-forms upon the Tree of Life are generally defined as follows, though there are a number of variants or alternatives, and no rigid or dogmatic formula.

1. Gods of the land, of nature, of Earth. May include heroes, ancestral beings, fairies, and spirits of nature.
2. Lunar gods, ancestral deities, and certain older gods of water. May include heroes, and inner-world or otherworld male images that embody divine forces.
3. Mercury, the messenger god. Hermes, the Hermetic tradition.
4. Gods of the emotion and feeling: Orpheus, the Orphic tradition.
5. Apollo, solar deities. The Son or Child of Light. Gods of harmony, therapy, balance. The Sacred Kings and redeeming figures of world religion.
6. Mars: gods of taking, death, vigor, martial skills, and the transition between death and life. Gods of hunting, culling, herding and animals breeding appear here in a higher octave or form than that of the earthly expressions.
7. Jupiter: the god of giving, creativity, outpouring energy, joy, mercy, and compassion.
8. Saturn: the dark brooding gods, lords of endless time, mediators of grief and suffering, deep cosmic tides of change.
9. The Zodiac: deities or mythic images associated with the 12 signs of the pattern of heaven. Stellar deities in groups or holisms. Also identified with Neptune/Poseidon, not simply as a sea god but as a great god of the stellar ocean. Functions of ferrying, wisdom, transition and enlightenment and awareness beyond death and beyond human personality are found here.
10. Ultimate Being, the first God. Identified sometimes with Uranus, the father of all gods, and of course with the orthodox concept of God in formal religion.

In our next chapter, we define and explore a detailed work program for the Male Mysteries, moving from theory and discussion to intense practice.

CHAPTER 10

Empowerment and transformation

A detailed work program

Using visualization/meditation/ceremony for empowerment
and transformation

The Five Branches pattern may be utilized and activated in a variety of different ways. A basic training and self-initiation program is possible, for either the individual or a small working group. In the ancient magical initiations of the Mysteries, the scenarios, patterns and archetypes, gods and goddesses, were ritually enacted as colorful and potent ceremonies. This may still be done today, providing we are realistic and allow for considerable changes of culture and consciousness, but as a basic modern method of working we may use regular repeated envisioning, for that which is in the imagination may become realized.

Through active use of the imagination with each of the Branches, we cause a response, a resonance, of the energies within ourselves connected to each Branch. Furthermore, there is a broad correspondence between the Five Branches and the subtle energies and physical organs of the male body. There is no need to make detailed correlations or so-called definitive connections on this level, as the correspondence will vary somewhat from person to person. Furthermore, the energy centers and their activation will vary during a lifetime, or even during the passage of a few hours of the day in some cases. This motion of the energy centers is seldom taken into account in rigid correspondences of chakras and subtle energies as published in most books. Some individuals, for example, need to liberate and enable movement of their energy centers, while others need quite the opposite and require a fixing and stabilizing of their energies. The popular idea that we must link up and activate our energy centers (chakras) is simplistic when it is taken out of the context of the profound traditions from which it comes.

The general pattern of the Five Branches of Warrior, Poet, Prophet Priest, and King in relation to the male body, and subtle energies is shown in Figure 6.

Our suggested working timetable (see Figure 7) uses the lunar cycle of energies, which affects both men and women strongly, as it does all life forms on the planet. This tidal cycle is more obviously known to women through the cycle of menstruation, but re-attuning to lunar cycles, or more accurately becoming properly aware of their presence within yourself, is an invaluable harmonizing and transforming process for men.

With the methods described here we do not need to concern ourselves overmuch with the state of our subtle energies at commencement. Too much introspective or intellectual concern over whether one's energies are fixed, fluid, rigid, or loose, is usually a distraction or even an evasion of the true work within one's self. The patterns and sequences of imaginative encounters in the exercises which follow will, of their own accord, act in a balancing and transformative way upon each of the Five Branches within ourselves, thus balancing and empowering the associated energies of the organism.

It is inevitable in any discussion of inner forces that the boundaries between images or seeming entities or archetypes, and the energies that they embody, become blurred or perhaps a better term might be softened. As a general rule the method works simply by regarding the beings, entities or archetypes as real, and not as symbols or explanations of energies within oneself. The key to this circular debate or riddle is to consider your own entity—are you a being, an image, or subtle energy? The answer to all of these questions is "yes."

The Three Thresholds

Development through imagination in the Male Mysteries can be defined in several stages, with an overall threefold pattern. The three main stages are termed the Three Thresholds, to give a clear definition of their function. They also resonate with the triplicity of the Three Faces of the God in myth and legend, and with the Three Mothers.

Within each of the Three Thresholds is another threefold pattern, three lesser thresholds or stages of development, giving a total of nine in all. We shall work through each of these stages, crossing each threshold, small and great, through direct visionary work. Remember that the visions trigger the subtle forces, and that they are not the forces themselves, but keys. The method is much simpler to undertake and experience than it sounds when described in a summary of this sort, as each of the lesser and greater thresholds merge harmonically with one another. An analogy might be that we do not need to think about every part of the body to walk ... yet walking moves the whole body.

We will consider (in Chapter 11) how envisioning might be practically enacted by a small group of men taking each of the roles in turn. Basic familiarity and practice of the imaginative and visionary aspects of the method should be established before working with the group enactment method. Without the basic visualization and familiarity with the symbols, imaginative beings, and energies involved, the psychodramatic or ritual method cannot be fully developed by an independent group. Please note that the emphasis here is that there is no authority or guru in such a group. The King is in ourselves, the Worker or primal Man ennobled, and is not a human authority figure.

The Room with Four Doors

We will be working within a well-established scenario, which involves imagining a room or chamber and then entering it. Such scenarios have been used for centuries in the spiritual, magical, mystical, or primal initiatory arts, and carry within them considerable power. Through gentle repetition of such exercises we are able to attune to them, and benefit from them. There is no suggestion here of remarkable willpower or intense concentration—while basic concentration is indeed necessary for visualizing, excessive effort will actually slow your development.

126 CELEBRATING THE MALE MYSTERIES

The powers of the imagination tend to develop through relaxed disciplined repetition rather than a mental equivalent of extreme weightlifting.

Building the room

The work begins by relaxing, eyes closed, breathing steadily, and calming your mind. (The exercise of Silence, Appendix 1, is recommended for this purpose.) The next stage is to build an image of a room: the shape of this room is shown in Figure 8 and should be carefully studied and remembered, as you will build this shape into a series of visualizations. The geometric shape has special qualities.

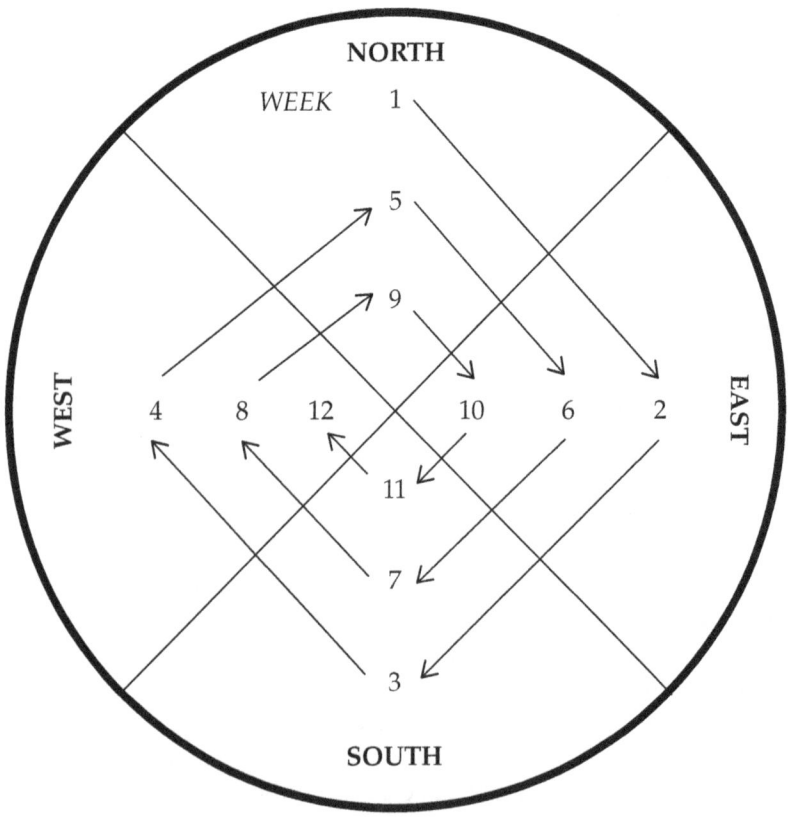

Figure 7: The 12-week cycle.

EMPOWERMENT AND TRANSFORMATION

This 12-fold cycle is recommended as the basic pattern for a work program of meditation and vision in the Male Mysteries. It may also be used, like our other figures, as a guideline for cycles of movement or sacred dance combined with visualization.

The cycle turns for 12 weeks if a lunar pattern is followed, and this is particularly helpful for modern men who have lost contact with their inherent relationship to natural rhythms. There is a popular delusion that males are solar and females lunar in rhythm, partly due to patriarchal propaganda and ignorance. Both men and women are affected by lunar and solar cycles, and our powers of imagination linked to sexual energies and life forces are enhanced by attuning consciously to a lunar cycle.

As a solar cycle, the 12-fold rhythm will take one year, or 12 hours of 12 consecutive days. For practical work, the lunar cycle is recommended first before working to the longer or shorter time scales.

The Cycle of Encounters with Companions, Goddesses, and Gods

```
TIME:   Week One   Week Two   Week Three   Week Four
           I          I           I            I         I
MOON:   Dark       Waxing     Full         Waning     Dark
```

(Begin the second phase in Week Five, third phase in Week Nine.)

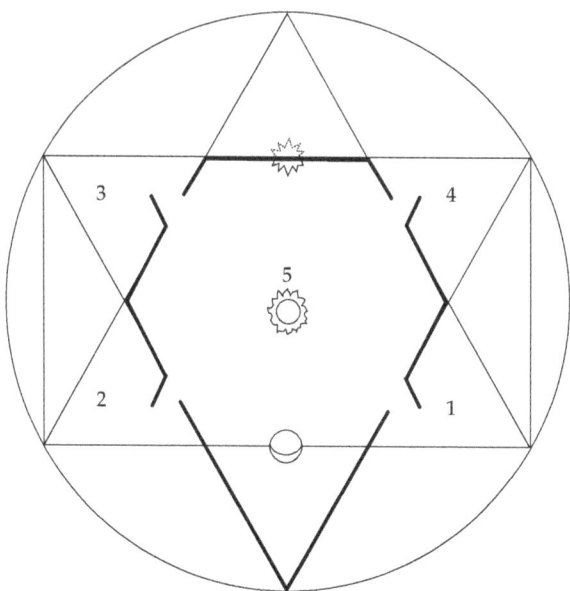

Figure 8: The Room with Four Doors.

The Room is a form of Sacred Space, a defined location in which energies and consciousness work. We see classic examples of this in temples and worship sites, ranging from prehistoric to modern. These physical forms of Sacred Space, be they stone circles or cathedrals, attune energies of many kinds, harmonizing geomantic or natural forces with those of humanity.

In visualization, the model of a room is particularly powerful, with differing effects depending upon its shape. The envisioned space may be located within a physical space which is a room of any suitable shape, or entirely within a regular rhythm of imaginative work upon inner levels.

Five is the number of man (see Figures 5 and 6), hence the use of a pentagonal room. This is located within an implicit hexagonal shape (see Figure 4), which is in turn within the Fourfold Circle (see Figure 1). The Four Companions—Warrior, Poet, Prophet and Priest—are encountered through Four Doors (see Chapter 10). Three Thresholds or octaves of transformation and encounter are possible through using the Room as a model for shaping consciousness and energy: The Companions, The Goddesses, The Gods.

1 = Warrior
2 = Poet
3 = Prophet
4 = Priest
5 = King

It is a very plain room with five walls. You sit at one end of the room, building its image around you. To your right and left are two walls that angle together to meet *behind* you. Before you are two further right and left hand walls, sloping in toward the fifth and smallest wall at the far end of the room. This fifth wall is a mirror, and in it you see a reflection of the four angled walls of the room, with yourself sitting in the furthest corner where the walls meet. On each of the four walls to your right and left is a door.

You enter into this image, feeling a sense of calm expectation. After a short period, you gently dissolve the image of the room, open your eyes, and return to your surroundings. Nothing else at this stage. If spontaneous visionary experiences happen, simply be still and observe. Do not engage, but always go into Stillness. There will be plenty of engagement soon!

Notes

1. This simple form is the foundation for the entire pattern of initiation through the Five Branches. It should be repeated several times, without strain or determination, until the feeling of the room and of being within it is established. Do not rush into the later stages of the visualizations until this basic image of the room is established, and you can pass in and out of it without great difficulty. Without great difficulty means that you should be able to imagine being in the room and to hold that image and feeling for a few minutes. There is no requirement that it becomes an alternative reality or that the image must be absolutely firm for long periods of time. You will find that the duration of the vision and the alternative reality of the room build naturally, particularly when you work in the later stages when the room becomes populated.
2. The Doors and Mirror. It is often found while working with this type of empowered image, that you are attracted to certain doors or to study yourself in the mirror. As a general rule, you should calmly relax out of such initial attractions. You may find the reverse, of course, for some people find the doors threatening or difficult to imagine and envision. It is also quite common to fail to see yourself in the mirror, or to see a distorted image. As discussed in our earlier chapters, the Mysteries do not use free association or similar techniques found in modern therapies. It is the actual shape of the room, and in the latter stages, the occupants, that are important in this type of work, not free associative reactions, attractions, or personal or subjective impressions.

    Simplicity is always the key to this initial stage of the work. By breathing steadily and relaxing it is possible to establish the basic image of the room, doors, and mirror, without entering into any activity or distraction. Building the room, dissolving it, rebuilding it ... dissolving it. That is all that is required at this stage.
3. Breathing and Imaging. You may find it helpful to breathe steadily in and out (no breath-holding or unusual breathing exercises or postures are necessary for this) and count breaths. A typical pattern might be to count ten steady breaths in and out while building the image of the room, two breaths for each wall, for example. Then a dissolving of the image for the space of three breaths in and out. This method may help if you have difficulty in initially building the image, but it must not become obsessive or rigid; that would undermine the work

130 CELEBRATING THE MALE MYSTERIES

in hand. Eventually, your breathing becomes unconscious and natural again in the later stages of the visualizations, so dependence upon counting breaths is merely a trick or interim stage.

Encountering the Five Branches

The Warrior

First, we build the image of the Room with Four Doors. We find ourselves in the room, with its mirror on the far wall, and four plain doors, each one being closed. We look at the floor of the room, and see three symbols inlaid in metal onto the floor (see Figure 9 for these inlaid symbols).

Figure 9: The three emblems.

Working within Sacred Space, the Pentagonal Room has Three Thresholds, each defined by a point of location within the space. By moving physically and through inner vision, we enable our crossing of these thresholds, and our encounters with the Companions, Goddesses and Gods, of the Male Mysteries. We begin at the entrance and exit point of the room, where all energies manifest as the physical body; all Companions, Goddesses and Gods manifest through the physical body.

The first threshold is broadly defined as Lunar consciousness, and this is where we begin when we enter into meditation and visualization for the first time, or upon the first level of altered awareness. This involves encounters with the Poet and Warrior, the Right and Left Hand energies and entities of male mental and emotional being. The Poet and Warrior enable us to proceed to the center of the room, the second threshold, or Solar consciousness.

The second threshold of altered awareness is where we meet the Prophet and Priest, the Right and Left Hand entities of male spiritual and transpersonal being. They enable us to proceed to the third threshold, broadly defined as Stellar consciousness. At the second threshold of Solar consciousness, we are in the center of the Sacred Space, balanced by all Four Companions. This is the first point or center of Kingship. Two further central points are found, through crossing the consciousness and energy thresholds of the four Goddesses and then of the Four Gods (see Chapter 10).

The Threshold of Stellar consciousness marks the transition or mirror between one level of the room and the next.

The first one is of silver, in the pattern of the full and crescent Moon, and is nearest to us. The second one is of gold, in the shape of the flaming Sun; this is in the center of the room. The third symbol merges into the base of the mirror—we see half of it, a radiating star of varied colors, while the other half is reflected in the mirror to complete the image. We pause and consider these three symbols, meditating upon them for a few moments.

Now we stand upright, and taking three paces forward, find that our feet rest upon the first emblem. As we touch it we hear a door opening behind us to the right. Looking only in the mirror ahead (not turning around), we see that a Warrior has emerged from that door, and he stands just behind our right shoulder. We look upon him in the mirror, and know that he has come first to protect us during our training, but more important to share his skill and knowledge with us, so that we will develop as warriors ourselves.

[In practice some men may feel wary of the Warrior, as if he has come to challenge or oppose. This is not unusual, as men have been conditioned to see one another as rivals, even when they are brothers of any kind. Working through the form several times without strenuous effort will usually reduce the reaction. If it becomes an enduring situation, take a break for a day, and go into Silence. Then begin again. Eventually, the reaction, which is within us, not in the Warrior, will come into balance. Repetition of the forms offered here, simply and calmly going through the program, repeating it, will gradually improve the effects. Like any skill that requires training, envisioning within the Mystery benefits from simple repetition and self-discipline.]

We pause in silence, feeling the presence of the warrior as he stands at our right shoulder. Here a pause is made for communion. The timing of this is judged separately on each occasion.

Now the Warrior turns and passes through his door. As the door closes, we step back from the Moon mark, and return to the end of the room. Now we slowly dissolve the image of the room, and emerge to our regular surroundings.

Notes

1. The usual method in this type of work is to see the inner-world contacts or archetypes in the mirror, without turning around. This technique greatly assists the appearance of the inner-world beings. The type of Warrior is not predefined in this vision, nor are the images of the other Branches, as the Warrior that appears in the mirror will be of the type most suited to your own needs and work.
2. The Presence of the Inner Warrior. The length of this sense of presence is left entirely to your own judgment, though it is usually fairly short to start with. It is not unusual during this silent phase for the sense of actual presence to greatly intensify, and for a flow of wordless communication and energy to occur. The inner-world Warrior empowers our physical energies and skills, our will, our endurance. He will also teach or enable development of the senses through special training techniques, and will often communicate matters concerned with our physical health and fitness. The Warrior also instills a sense of honor, charity and tempering of power to favor and assist others, even at the expense of one's self-interest.
3. The Departure. You may find that the Warrior departs of his own accord, or alternatively you should slowly withdraw from

the sense of communication when you are ready. Some men will find that it is easier to withdraw from the room while the Warrior remains within it. On leaving the room, you should make notes briefly describing your experience. In many cases, the inner-world contact gives you something within the vision. If this occurs, note what it is and draw it, if it is unusual (which is often the case). Such gifts are later used as meditative tools or emblems in their own right, encapsulating the entire experience into one powerful key image. These are a type of magical implement, and may have physical counterparts.

Encountering the Poet

First, we build the image of the Room with Four Doors, and finding ourselves within this room, take three paces forward to the first emblem upon the floor, inlaid as a silver full and crescent Moon.

As our feet touch the mark, we hear a door open behind us to our left. Looking in the mirror on the far wall, we see a Poet (or Bard) enter the room, behind our left shoulder. Looking upon him, we know that he has come to give us inspiration, and that he will share his skill and knowledge with us, so that our own power of poetry, memory, and feeling will develop steadily. Poetry: skill at expressing our thoughts and inspirations. Memory: reliance upon our own unique consciousness, unaided by any mechanical, electronic, or digital devices. Feeling: increasing ability to understand what and how we feel our emotions.

We pause in silence, feeling the presence of the Poet as he stands at our left shoulder. [A pause for silent communion here.] Now the Poet turns and passes through his door. As the door closes we step back from the Moon mark, and return to the end of the room. Now we slowly dissolve the image of the room, and emerge to our regular surroundings.

Notes

1. The presence of the Poet or Bard uplifts our inspirations, feelings, and sensitivity. Inner-world poets, however, are not wilting sensitive types; if they appear as true Poets or Bards, they are men of considerable power, acting as storehouses and teachers of vast collections of wisdom, music, song, poetry and magical traditions.

2. While the magic of the Warrior is that of developing disciplines of both strength and flexibility of mind and body, the magic of the Poet is that of developing the arts of inspiration, memory, and the feelings. Each Branch has its own stream or teaching of magic, in which accessible outer skills merge imperceptibly into unusual abilities and raise the level of consciousness and power.

The Second Threshold: encountering the Prophet

We begin by entering the Room with Four Doors. When we are within the room, in our inner vision, we step up to the first mark, the emblem of the Moon in the floor. As we do so, two doors open behind us, and in the Mirror ahead we see our Warrior and Poet come into the room, and stand on either side, just behind us.

Now we begin a gradual progression into the center of the room, with three steps to the emblem of the Sun set in gold on the floor. As we take the first step, the Mirror on the far wall clouds over until we cannot see the Warrior and Poet, nor can we see ourselves. Suddenly a nameless fear enters us, taking the form of personal doubts, worries, and insecurities. Just as we are about to step back, we feel a firm hand on our right shoulder. The Warrior whispers a word in our ear […] [this word is heard only by you] As he does so we find that we are filled with a share of the power of the Warrior, and we know that it is becoming our own Power.

We take the Second Step and feel another hand upon our left shoulder, as the Poet whispers a word in our ear […]. As he does so we are filled with a share of the knowledge, perception, and feeling of the Poet, and it becomes our own knowledge, perception, and feeling.

The Mirror clears, and we take the Third Step forward to stand upon the central Solar emblem. The Warrior and Poet step back, and for a moment we stand alone, waiting ready. [Pause for silent meditation here.]

Immediately to our left is a door. It slowly opens, and a Prophet enters the room to stand before us, on our left hand side. In the mirror, we see reflections of the Warrior and Poet, and ourselves, but the Prophet we see directly before us. He looks into our eyes, and a silent communication passes between him and us. [Silent communion here.]

After the communion phase, step backward to the first emblem, and repeat the sequence for exiting the room as before.

Encountering the Priest

We begin by entering the Room with Four Doors. When we are within the room, in our inner vision, we step up to the first mark, the emblem of the Moon in the floor. As we do so, two doors open behind us, and in the Mirror ahead we see our Warrior and Poet come into the room and stand on either side, just behind us.

We now intend to step into the center of the room, to the emblem of the Sun set in gold on the floor. As we take the first step, the Mirror on the far wall clouds over until we cannot see the Warrior and Poet, nor can we see ourselves. Suddenly a nameless fear enters us, and takes the form of personal doubts, worries, and insecurities. Just as we are about to step back, we feel a firm hand on our right shoulder. The Warrior whispers a word in our ear […], and as he does so we find that we are filled with a share of the power of the Warrior, and we know that it is our own Power. We feel another hand upon our left shoulder, and the Poet whispers a word in our ear […] as he does so we are filled with a share of the knowledge, perception, and feeling of the Poet, and it is our own knowledge, perception, and feeling.

The Mirror clears and we take three firm paces forward to stand upon the central emblem. The Warrior and Poet step back and for a moment we stand alone, waiting ready. [Pause for silent meditation here.]

Immediately to our right is a door. It slowly opens and a Priest enters the room to stand before us on our right hand side. In the mirror, we see reflections of the Warrior and Poet, and ourselves, but the Priest we see directly before us. He looks into our eyes, and a silent communication passes between him and us. [Silent communication here.]

Repeat the exit sequence as before.

Notes

On returning to outer consciousness, the usual notes are taken. There should be a pause of one day after the encounter of the Prophet and Priest (see Figure 7 for potential time scales of working with these exercises).

What should they look like?

In this series of visualizations, members of the Branches are not described in detail, as they will appear differently for each individual.

Nor is there any requirement that your Warrior, Poet, Priest, and Prophet be of the same time period, culture, or type. There seems to be a general rule with this type of imaginative inner work that the contacts appear in the form of people from the ancestral past. A further general but not inflexible rule is that they are from cultures that relate in some way to your own, either ancestrally or in terms of general tradition and consciousness.

Although the general rule and experience is that the inner contacts or people seem to be from the ancestral past or from past idealized societies or places, there is no reason why they should not be from other worlds altogether or even from the future. Having said this, I would stress very strongly that prudence is necessary in this respect as the entire experience must never be allowed to degenerate into whimsy or fantasy. Images from popular entertainment such as films, television, science fiction, and so forth are emphatically not in the mainstream of the Mysteries, and can even be misleading and weakening under obsessive or flippant circumstances. This is not role-playing or fantasy gaming.

The general rule is that the contacts are from the ancestral or cultural past because there is a connection between the deeper more potent levels of consciousness and energy and the apparent flow of historical time. The deeper we go within ourselves, the more we seem to link to past humanity and to other life forms. Hence future contacts are rare, while contact with beings from other worlds altogether may be less rare but are often difficult to cope with or are potentially confusing. The value of spiritual or consciousness-changing traditions is that they give enormous flexibility within certain simple and known parameters. If we stay within these parameters the changes are certain to occur.

For Westerners, this broadly ancestral or cultural stream of contact can produce a surprisingly wide range of inner-world people, including those from virtually unknown past civilizations, simple ancestral societies, and in some cases contacts that appear to be definable in terms of more recent modern history. Eastern societies still have a vast range of mythic entities well defined in tradition and religion, and so Eastern inner contacts tend to work through such well-known forms.

Those of us who are of the many races from around the world, but living within the broad range of what is still called Western civilization, are able to draw upon a mixed range of inner contacts and will eventually need to settle into an ancestral or specific stream of energy that satisfies both intellectual and intuitive needs. This can only come through experience, hence the need for all types of people within the Mysteries, regardless of their roots, to have open and flexible techniques that are not attuned to rigid teachings, dogmas, predetermined images or limited inner-world or religious beings.

While working through these exercises, it would be harmonious to find that each of the Five Branches was, say, a persona from Ancient Greece or that they epitomized the Four Directions or noble castes of Celtic primal culture. In practice, this seldom happens; do not be too surprised if your Poet and Warrior, Prophet and Priest, are from seemingly different times and cultures. In most working patterns, the inner-world contacts remain constant, but there are occasional instances where the contact will spontaneously change appearance or personality during the higher levels of empowered working. If such a change occurs, it needs to be carefully assessed, and if necessary the next session can be addressed either to your original contact or to the new one. If you seek your first contact, and he is always replaced by the further contact or persona, then this second form is the new archetype or inner-world contact for your new level of consciousness and energy.

In working the Mystery, a major change of consciousness and energy is embodied by the change from working with the representative of a specified Branch (Warrior, Poet, etc.) through to working with the god or goddess behind that Branch. This change or octave transformation is steered to a certain extent by the progressive structure of the visions and the working pattern defined in our set of exercises.

The sleeping King: awakening, healing, and crowning

The cycle of visions and encounters

Our basic working pattern is founded upon a 12-week cycle, divided into three lunar months. The lunar synchronization is not essential but is easy to follow, and will enhance the subtle energies that arise within such regular visionary and transformative exercises.

The three cycles are:

1. Encountering the Branches.
2. Encountering the Goddesses.
3. Encountering the Gods.

The twelve-week pattern involves the Three Thresholds, each of which has a holism or minor cycle or rhythm within it. This cyclic rhythmic work is very beneficial, particularly when linked to the natural lunar cycle, as it re-establishes basic energy patterns within us, those from which men in particular have become separated to their disadvantage. Within each cycle, the separate parts are, in themselves, simple visions which that lead us toward the culmination and completion of the cycle. There is no requirement, however, that you force your way through all three major cycles if you are averse to doing so. The first cycle, encountering the Branches of Warrior, Poet, Prophet, and Priest may be repeated as often as you wish before moving on to the second one.

The cycle of encountering the goddesses, however, should come before attempting the cycle of encountering the gods, as this is how men achieve maturity and balance with the more powerful forces of the Mysteries. The first cycle will, of its own accord, go a long way toward awakening our energies. There is an important correlation between the three cycles, and the major myth of the sleeping and wounded King found in many forms worldwide and directly relevant to the Male Mysteries.

The sleeping and wounded King

In various legends, we find the theme of the sleeping and wounded King. The basic story is that a King has been wounded deeply, and is in a coma or sleep somewhere between life and death.

Many powerful myths and rituals revolve around finding and awakening the sleeping King, and how he many recover wholeness. Even orthodox Christianity is firmly based upon a death and resurrection myth. In Arthurian legend, for an example, with both Christian and pagan Celtic roots, the wounded Arthur is carried away over the sea to a magical island, where the goddess of healing and rebirth will restore him to life at the time of greatest need for his people.

This myth has an analogy in all humans, male or female, but we are concerned here with its specific relevance to the Male Mysteries. The man entering the Mysteries is both a primal worker and a sleeping wounded King. The King must be awakened, healed, and finally crowned. These three stages of transformation correspond to the three cycles of the Mystery as follows:

1. Awakening the sleeping King: Encountering the Four Branches.
2. Healing his wounds: Encountering the Four Goddesses.
3. Crowning in full realization: Encountering the Four Gods.

In each cycle, the Fifth Branch, King or Worker, is always ourselves. The same cycle would work in a Women's Mystery as follows:

1. Encountering the Four Companion or Sister Branches of Womanhood.
2. Encountering the Gods.
3. Encountering the Goddesses.

A 12-week working timetable

This variable timetable should be regarded only as a general guide, and not as a rigid schedule. The order of development is important, and should not be jumped through or altered, but the time scale for each Branch and for the later deeper encounters will vary according to the individual or group. The best procedure would be to adopt the short time scale suggested here initially, but to expand or contract any longer time cycles according to need, intuition, and growing experience. The Mysteries, or any inner training, be it magical or spiritual or a combination of both, are not hobbies or temporary interests. Knowing Yourself is the task of a lifetime. Changing Yourself, however, is an ever-present potential.

Short time scale

1. Building the Room with Four Doors
   This exercise should be done daily; once per day is enough, but twice would be more effective. The envisioning should be done at the same time and if possible in the same location every day. This is an individual training exercise, regardless of any group work. When the building of the room has become reasonably effective, you should proceed to the next stage of the work.
2. The people in the room
   The first encounters are undertaken singly: the Warrior first, then the Poet. This order may be reversed if necessary, though the order of the next encounters, those of Prophet and Priest would normally remain. A basic short timetable would be as follows:

Day 1: The Warrior (duration variable).
Day 2: The Poet (duration variable).
Day 3: Pause and rest. Note any dreams or intimations that seem to be connected to the workings. Do not push or rush into the next stage without this break.
Day 4: The Prophet (duration variable).
Day 5: The Priest (duration variable).
Day 6: Pause (as in Day 3 above).
Day 7: Begin the cycle again with the vision of an empty room, then proceed again from Day 1 to Day 6.

The cycle of encountering the Warrior/Poet/Prophet/Priest takes one week. It should be worked through as an ideal cycle of three times, thus taking three weeks, with approximately 30 minutes per day. You would then break and rest for the fourth week of the month. Men often find that this routine affects their dreams.

Lunar timing

Ideally this cycle should match the lunar cycle, which has a regular effect on the life energies of all beings on Earth. To fit the working in this manner, simply calculate backward from the dark of the Moon, letting that be at the end of the fourth week, the resting week. This means that the full Moon will be approximately at the end of the second cycle or week of encounters (see Figure 7).

The Four Goddesses

You enter the Room with Four Doors, and immediately the Poet and Warrior enter and join you. Together you step toward the center of the chamber, and stand upon the second emblem, the image of the Sun set in gold into the floor. The Warrior and Poet stand behind you to the right and left. As you step onto the emblem, the Prophet and Priest emerge from the two doors in front of you, and stand before you. You are now in the center of the room, in the center of a square, marked at each corner by Four Companions, the Warrior, the Poet, the Prophet, and the Priest. It is time to step forward three paces to the third and last emblem, embedded into the mirror wall ahead, half in the room, half reflected in the mirror.

You formulate your will to step forward, and feel a nameless and formless fear, a degree of pure panic, causing your hair to rise and your skin to crawl. You feel a presence in the chamber standing directly before you, and know that this as the presence of the Guardian of all Thresholds. He forbids you to step further.

Now the Prophet and the Priest step closer, and the Prophet places one hand upon the small of your back. The Priest places one hand upon the top of your head, and you feel a flow of energy like fire run up your spine. The Poet and Warrior each take your elbows in a firm grip, and as all four support you, you feel a sense of weightlessness and ecstasy. [Pause here for a short meditation.]

Suddenly the Four Companions throw you forward into the mirror: the shock of this movement dispels the sense of panic, and you pass right through the mirror into the reflected room beyond. [Brief pause here.]

Encountering the First Goddess

This room is empty, and is the mirror image of the one that you have left. There are four walls with doors in them, tapering to a narrow point at the far end of the room. You know that to return to your outer consciousness, you must cross this room, and leave from the far side. There are no emblems on the floor of the room, and it is silent, waiting. [Pause here.]

You feel awake, alert, ready, yet uncertain of what will happen in this empty room. Cautiously you take a step forward into the chamber, until the first pair of doors are on your right and left. As you do so, the door on your right opens, and a Warrior Goddess emerges from it.

The Warrior Goddess is tall and vigorous; she carries a sharp-pointed spear. A portion of her long red hair is brushed up and fixed into a tall crest, while the rest flows down her back like the mane of a horse. Her face is beautiful and savage and she looks directly into your eyes, challenging you to reveal your skill and potential. As she looks at you, you feel the inner fire aroused by the touch of the Priest and Prophet burning within your blood and rising to your head. As it rises, the Warrior Goddess lifts her spear above her head in a sign of victory. Then she begins to weave a circle dance around you, making many turns and twists. As she does so, you feel her awareness within your own, and must stand in stillness, communing with her power. [Silent contemplation here.]

Now the Warrior Goddess pauses in her dance, and stands directly before you, looking down at you. She holds a token or gift in one hand, and gives this to you. She steps aside and motions that you must walk to the far end of the room. As you do so, you see a familiar chair in that far corner, and as you turn to sit upon it you discover that the Goddess has vanished. You sit, and look at the pattern of the room, with the mirror on the far wall. Now you quietly dissolve the room, and return to your outer awareness.

Encountering the Second Goddess

(At this stage, the individual may choose how to proceed. He may work directly with the reversed or Second Room, by building the room as it appears after passing through the mirror. Alternatively, he may use the visualization in which the Four Companions pass him through the mirror into the empty room. If in doubt, or if you try the more direct method and it does not seem to work fully, repeat the vision of passing through the mirror.)

A historical note: the double chamber of initiation was used physically in some ritual lodges. If such a chamber can be built or adapted, the methods can be combined into a group ritual. This should only be undertaken by a group of men who have done the initial work in vision until they are sure of its dynamics.

Upon entering and standing in the Second Room, you hear a door open to your left. You turn to look in that direction, and see a Goddess of Inspiration and Intuition.

She holds a tiny flame in her cupped hands, and she seems to flow and change color as you look upon her. She looks into your eyes and the flame in her hands suddenly flashes and rises up; as it does so, you feel the inner fire rising up your spine. [Pause here.] Slowly she begins to circle around you, and as she moves you feel a flow of ideas, concepts, intuitions, attuning to your own awareness. As her movement increases in speed, her changing colors seem to flow into a pattern of light, and you pause to contemplate her presence. [Silent pause here.]

Now the Goddess of Inspiration and Intuition stands before you, and gives you a token or gift. She indicates that you should move to the far end of the room, where you see a familiar chair. As you turn to sit in this chair, you hear a door closing. Now you are alone in a familiar room, and slowly you return to outer consciousness.

Encountering the Third Goddess

You enter the Second Room, and stand in the center. The room is very empty and still, the Four Doors remain closed. As you stand in silent meditation in the center of the still room, you feel a slight movement beneath your feet, as if the ground is trembling. Gradually you become aware of an energy arising from beneath, up out of the ground below, through the floor, through your feet and into your body. This is the power of the Goddess of the Land.

As the power rises through your body, it reaches your genitals, and triggers a powerful sexual desire. As you feel this desire, the door on your left opens and an aged crone enters the room. She slowly raises her left hand and your intense sexual desire increases until the energy begins to rise upwards toward your heart.

The Goddess of the Land fills you with both desire and aversion, longing, fear, and deep respect. You do not know what to do. She steps close to you and looks into your eyes. A wordless communion passes between you. [Silent pause here.]

Now images of the primal land emerge in your vision, the pure timeless land, uncorrupted, un-abused, and you know that you will give your life to restore that land if the Goddess asks you to do so.

She lays her withered hand upon your throat, and you feel the intense sexual desire rise like a breath of wind to impel your voice to speak. You utter the words that come freely […] [spontaneous words uttered here.]

As you speak, you see the crone change into a young woman of calm appearance and great beauty; she smiles upon you, and the sexual desire gently harmonizes into a feeling of peace and fulfillment. The Goddess of the Land indicates a chair at the far end of the room, and you walk toward it. As you turn to sit, you hear a door closing behind you. Now you return to outer consciousness.

Encountering the Fourth Goddess

You enter the room, and as you do so the two doors to your right and left open simultaneously. The Warrior Goddess and the Inspiration Goddess enter the room and stand to your right and left, holding your elbows in a tight grip. They walk with you to the center of the room, and the third door on your left opens, and the aged crone enters the chamber. She stands directly in front of you, challenging you to proceed no further, for to take another step is to die. You speak the words that you uttered spontaneously when you first met her, and as you do so a great stillness descends upon the room. [Silent pause here.]

From deep beneath the floor, seeming to come from within the heart of the Earth itself, a slow resonant drum beat sounds. The three goddesses step away from you and begin to move slowly with this beat, circling around you in a grave and stately weaving dance. With each step, their shape and age and color changes.

Gradually the speed increases, and the drumming intensifies. The three figures now whirl and spin about in a blur of color, a host of changing faces. Within these faces, you see momentarily your own grandmother, mothers, sisters, your lovers, and many more familiar beloved yet unknown to you.

The beating drum rises to a rapid continuous throbbing sound, and suddenly stops. The shape-changing host of women rushes in upon you, and resolves into three goddesses, the Goddess of the Land, the Goddess of Inspiration, and the Goddess of Warriors. Each one carries in her hand a different colored sword, and for an instant it seems that they will cut off your head. You stand still, awaiting whatever will come. [Silent pause here.]

The three goddesses disappear, and the fourth door stands open. Through it, you see the depth of space filled with swirling stars. In the center of that vastness is a slowly spiraling cloud of silver gray and white, shot through with many flashes of color. A figure, wrapped in a dark robe with a deep hood pulled over her face slowly approaches you from within that spiral of stars. As she draws closer, your vision of her seems to cloud over, yet the sense of presence grows. Now her presence fills the room, yet she cannot be seen. You attend upon her in silent communion, for she is the Great Goddess of all Being. [Silent contemplation.]

Gradually you become aware of a quiet empty room, and yourself standing in the center of that room. Before you is a familiar chair, and you walk to this and sit. Now you return to outer awareness, leaving the Second Room behind.

The Four Gods

Before we move onto the envisioning for the Four Gods, a brief introduction to their nature and power should be given. Although we can find historical mythic content in the images used, and partly relate the god-forms to specific deities from the pantheons of various cultures, these are not cultural or historically defined gods. They are, in one sense, the gods behind the gods, and they are also the gods within each and every man. No man can come to the gods within until he has truly encountered the power of the Goddess.

In formal religion, gods and goddesses always tend toward an increasingly defined presentation; as a society develops and becomes more complex, so do the gods and goddesses rigidify and become less fluid. In the Mysteries, however, deeper aspects of deity were explored, the most important concept being that any god or goddess has a multifold nature. In our modern restoration of the Male Mysteries, the main god-forms, archetypes and images inherent within human consciousness and history are resolved into Four Gods. These in turn are unified into One Being. By working through this archetypical and magical pattern, a man comes to inner Kingship.

While much of this seems complex when described, the actual experience, given form by guided visualization and ritual pattern making, replaces thousands of words of exposition or analysis. Nevertheless, a short summary of the attributes of each of the Four Gods is helpful before we enter into the actual visionary sequences that enable us to contact their power directly. If you have worked through the encounters with the Four Companions and the Four Goddesses, the effect of what follows in this chapter will be very powerful indeed.

The nature of the Four Gods

Just as we encountered the Branches of Warrior, Poet, Prophet, and Priest as Companions, then as Goddesses, so do we encounter them as Gods. A god is a male-defined image for polarized universal power. But a god is not an analogy or a substitute; he is also a living entity, just as you and I are living entities. Never make the mistake of thinking that you are dealing with symbolism in this work—symbols are used to weave the fabric of the visualization, but the entities that populate it are real; possibly more real than ourselves, as their existence is not limited by serial time or corporeal cycles of birth and death. Let us briefly consider each of the Four Gods:

1. The Warrior God: a god of Compassion and Severity.
2. The Poet God: a god of Love and Death.
3. The Prophet God: a god of Reason and Madness.
4. The Priest God: a god of Light and Darkness.

All Four Gods merge in the central unity of the Divine Son, or in man as the sacred priest-king who mediates their forces to the land and to all living beings. The perfected goal of humanity is to mediate the awareness of all Being to all Being, and specifically to all beings in our own world, our Planet Earth.

To give some examples of cultural god-forms relating to Four Gods of the Branches, we would need to find at least two culturally defined deities for each of the four primal gods of the Mystery.

1. The Warriors' god of compassion and severity (life-giving/life-taking) finds cultural expression in deities such as Jupiter and Mars.
2. The Poets' god of love and death finds cultural expression in deities such as Orpheus, or in Celtic tradition Oenghus Og.
3. The Prophets' god of madness and reason finds cultural expression in deities such as Pan, Apollo, or in Celtic tradition Cernunnos and Mabon.
4. The priests' God of Light and Darkness finds cultural expression in deities such as Christ and the great Savior figures of world religion. Note that the light and darkness are not antagonistic but unified, each unable to Be without the other. Polarity out of Unity, Unity in Polarity.

In this last Branch, we find the Order of Sacred or Divine Kingship, best known today as defined in the Judeo-Christian Mystery as the Order of Melchizedek, but by no means limited to that variant.

As a general rule, the detailed appearance of the gods and goddesses has been left to your own inspiration and vision, though they are firmly within world traditions for such inner work. In some schools of inner development, both psychological and spiritual or magical, long and detailed descriptions of archetypes, gods and goddesses, or highly defined visualization scenarios are used extensively. In our method of working, however, the deeper and more potent the energies and forms, the less outer verbal definition is given to them.

This means in effect that if you attempt the deep stages of envisioning, those of the Four Gods, without working through the early stages of the Companions and the Goddesses, then you may find very little to work with. The appearance in power of the Four Gods comes as a result

EMPOWERMENT AND TRANSFORMATION 147

of working through the preceding sequence of visions; if you do so, the gods will unquestionably appear, and you will be able to see their appearance quite clearly, with your inner vision, your sacred faculty of empowered imagination.

More important than their image or appearance is the unique character and feeling of each of the Four Gods and their Directions. While descriptions of methods for the Mysteries are obliged to depend upon visual descriptions, such visions are only useful to lead us to feeling the presence of the gods. Some men have heightened visual imaginations; others are more likely to feel. Such feeling is a higher octave of the physical senses, especially touch.

The attributes of the Directions and of Sacred Space are shown in Figure 10, and these underpin the character of each of the Four Gods.

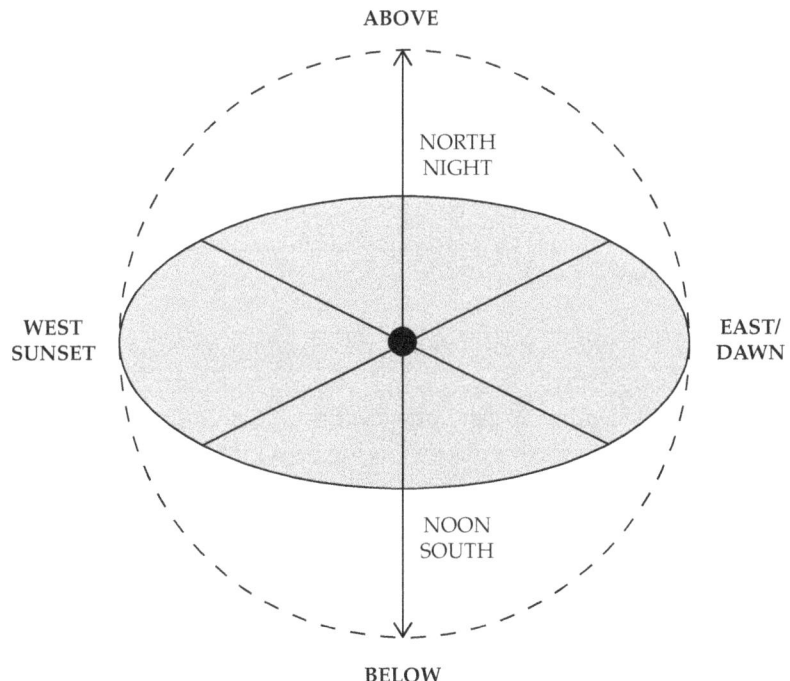

Figure 10: Sacred space.

Sacred Space is defined for us by the shape of a human being standing upon the surface of the land and planet. Seven Directions are aligned to: ABOVE/BELOW/WITHIN/EAST/SOUTH/WEST/NORTH. The resulting sphere is infinite or contracted to the smallest imaginable location.

Above is the sky and stellar universe, below is the land. Within is our center of existence, our primal and perfect Being.

The Four Directions of consciousness mirror the four planetary Directions, defined for us by the magnetic fields of the Earth, and our orbit around the Sun. A further definition of stellar Directions is through the movement of the Sun within the galaxy.

When we define awareness in Sacred Space, and align it to the Seven Directions, our energies and consciousness become increasingly balanced and enhanced. Sacred Space is alive with its own consciousness, and in meditation we find that Sacred Space responds and talks back to us, often in surprising ways.

In the manifest outer world all creatures occupy Sacred Space, and there is no such thing as inert matter. In the Mysteries, Sacred Space is populated by ourselves, by gods and goddesses, and often by heroes, ancestors, and a wide range of other beings, including companion creatures and non-human or non-organic entities. Many examples of this holism of beings occur in mythology, legend, and spiritual traditions.

Working with the Male Mysteries, we limit the People in the Sacred Space to those that have the most powerful effect upon men in meditation, vision, and Sacred Movement.

East

Dawn/Spring/Element of Air/ the Sword or Arrow/Powers of Life. The Warrior God/mediator of Life-Giving And Life-Taking.

South

Noon/Summer/Element of Fire/the Rod Staff or Spear/Powers of Light. The Priest-King's God/mediator of light and darkness.

West

Evening/Autumn/Element of Water/the Cup or Cauldron/Powers of Love. The Poet's God/mediator of Love and Sacrifice.

North

Midnight/Winter/Element of Earth/the Shield or Mirror/Powers of Law and Liberation. The Prophet's God/mediator of Reason and Madness.

Below

The Power of the Land and Planet/ultimately the Power of the Great Goddess of All Being.

Above

The Power of the Stars/ultimately the Power of the Great God of All Being.

Remember that there is no religious requirement in these terms, no orthodoxy, paganism, or any other kind of -ism. These are simply the age-old, universal terms that humanity has used, concepts to partially define that which has no rigid definitions. All that you need to do is work through the sequences described, and with practice the entire structure of the Mystery comes alive. If you are later able to dispose of it altogether and work directly with energies that these primal images and patterns arouse, then you will have fulfilled part of your quest to know yourself. For most of us, however, certain patterns and archetypes or imaginal forms are essential as keys to empowerment. They act just as any material tool or vehicle or musical instrument, or other vital living aid to skill and motion and balance works—the form is theirs, the skill to work with it is ours, and eventually we become independent of the means or vehicles, even though we can and do use them regularly.

Encountering the Gods

You enter the Second Room, which is empty and still. The Four Doors are closed. In the center of the room is a small circular altar or table, and you walk toward this. You stand with your palms resting upon the surface of this altar, and as you touch it the room seems to change shape and become a square, rotating until the Four Doors are located in new positions. One is before you in the East, one behind you in the West, one to your right in the South, and one to the left in the North. You meditate in silence upon the Four Directions, and wait for a door to open. [Silent pause here.]

Now the door in the East, directly before you opens, and a figure steps into its frame. He is the God of Life-Giving and Life-Taking, embodying the power of the perfect Warrior in all worlds. Look upon him and remember his appearance. [Period of silent meditation here, allowing the image to take form.]

Now the door in the West, behind you opens. You slowly step around the central altar, until you stand in the East, facing West. Framed in the doorway is a figure; he is the God of Perfect Love and Immaculate Death, embodying the power of the Poet in all worlds. Look upon him and remember his appearance. [Period of silent meditation here, allowing the image to take form.]

As you face West, you feel the power of the God of the East flow into you, until it seems you are the perfect Warrior looking upon the perfect Poet. Now you turn again and face East, and as you do so you feel the power of the God of the West flow into you, until it seems that you are the perfect Poet looking upon the perfect Warrior. You pause in communion with both gods, and their power brings harmony and fills your essential being. [Silent communion here.]

Slowly the power of the God of the East and the God of the West fades, and the door before you closes. You turn around the central altar, and the door in the West closes. You feel the room move back to a familiar shape, and in the far corner you see a chair. You step six paces to this chair, and sit. Now you return to outer consciousness slowly, taking your time over the transition. [Notes can be made at this stage.]

You enter the Second Room, which is empty and still. The Four Doors are closed. In the center of the room is a small circular altar or table, and you walk toward this. You stand with your palms resting upon the surface of this altar, and as you touch it the room seems to change shape and become a square, rotating until the Four Doors are located in new positions. One is before you in the East, one behind you in the West, one to your right in the South, and one on your left in the North. You meditate in silence upon the Four Directions, and wait for a door to open. [Silent pause here.]

You hear a door open on your left, and walk around the altar until you are facing North. A figure stands framed in the doorway: he is the god of madness and reason, embodying the power of the Prophet in all worlds. Look upon him and remember his appearance. [Period of silent meditation here, allowing the image to take form.]

Now you hear the door behind you in the South open. You step around the altar until you stand in the North facing South. A figure stands framed within the doorway, he is the god of light and darkness. Look upon him and remember his appearance. [Period of silent meditation here, allowing the image to take form.]

As you face the South, you feel the power of the god of the North flow into you until it seems that you are the perfect Prophet looking upon the perfect Priest. Now you step around the altar and stand in the South, facing North. You feel the power of the god of the South flow into you, until you are the perfect Priest looking upon the perfect Prophet.

Now the power of both gods is harmonized and merged within you, and you commune with them in silence. [Silent period for communion here.]

Slowly the power of the god of the North and the god of the South fades, and the door before you closes. You turn around the central altar, and the door in the South closes. You feel the room move back into its familiar shape, and in the far corner you see a chair. You step six paces to this chair, and sit. Now you return to outer consciousness slowly, taking your time over the transition. [Notes are made at this stage.]

You enter the Second Room, which is empty and still. The Four Doors are closed. In the center of the room is a small circular altar or table, and you walk toward this. You stand with your palms resting upon the surface of this altar, and as you touch it the room seems to change shape and become a square, rotating until the Four Doors are located in new positions. One is before you in the East, one behind you in the West, one to your right in the South, and one on your left in the North. You meditate in silence upon the Four Directions, and wait for a door to open. [Silent pause here.]

The Four Doors open simultaneously, and you feel the presence of the gods of the Four Directions enter the room and flow into you, until they are perfectly balanced within you. [Pause here.]

Now you feel a deep movement in the ground beneath your feet, and the Earth's power rises up and out of the land to ascend your spine. It rises to your genitals, and you utter the word given to you by the Goddess of the Land; it rises to your heart and you are filled with boundless love; it rises to your throat and you breathe the universal breath; it rises to your head and your mind is illuminated. As the power rises into your head, you feel the presence of a responding power from above you, radiating down into your body. You pause in silent communion as the forces from Below and Above merge within you, balanced and perfected by the gods of the Four Directions. [Silent contemplation here.]

Now you breathe deeply, and acknowledge the Gods of the Four Directions: in the East is the God of Warriors; in the West is the God of Poets; in the North is the God of Prophets; in the South is the God of Priests. In the depths is the power of the Great Mother, and in the height the power of the Star Father. In the center is a man, yourself. Be at peace with yourself in silence. [Pause here.]

Now the power from Above and Below has merged within you, and it slowly fades, entering every part of your body becoming absorbed within your entire being. It gradually reduces in intensity yet remains indwelling in every part of you, even in your bones and in your blood and in your cells. One by one, the Four Gods withdraw, from the East, from the West, from the South from the North. You stand alone and complete within a calm empty room. Now the Fourfold room dissolves, and you return to your outer life, ready to mediate the power that you have experienced to all that lives.

CHAPTER 11

Toward the future of the Male Mysteries

The reader with a sense of humor might well observe that this book has progressively dematerialized. We began with chapters on the historical and psychological progress, or lack of progress, of men's inner disciplines, arts, and potentials in post-Christian materialist Western culture. These arts and skills were then gradually redefined within a modern system incorporating many techniques from the ancient imaginative arts, magical and spiritual traditions, and from the inner Mysteries themselves.

At that stage, we began to move inwards, reaching beyond history and society, religion or psychology, into the seldom explored realms of energy and consciousness. The last stages of our visionary program, though simple, are potent. While having the most power, the last set of visualizations, those of the Four Gods, are also the briefest and least substantial or fully described of any in the book.

After an inner resolution of energies, after finding some degree, however modest, of realization, of unmasking, of Kingship, what happens then? The answer must be that we seek to re-materialize the entire Mystery, to let the inherent power within flow out through men into the natural world, to be shared by all that lives. There is a wide range of implications in terms of exercises and specific practices in this expression and sharing of the Mysteries.

The most interesting implications are that, given a number of people who have worked through the entire sequence of empowering vision to some effect, that this group might then work with other men toward sharing and expanding the changes of consciousness inherent in the Five Branches.

Throughout this book, the aim has been to make such direct work a real possibility, removing the concepts of development and initiation from the old and decidedly rotten stereotype of the adept or Master and pupil, or of the cunning all-knowledgeable therapist and wise man with an ignorant confused client or patient. Such stereotypes must be broken and dissolved if we are to truly grow, and their beautiful inner core is to be revealed.

There is a range of group techniques for men's awareness: do they go far enough into the true Male Mystery to carry forward into the future? We see typical examples in terms of group sharing of life stories, sweat-lodges, learning to forgive our fathers, to redevelop male brotherhood and trust, and so forth. While we can value such methods, particularly in the context of developing trust and group sharing in a society that is designed to make men hostile to one another at all levels, they do not begin to approach the deeper energies and transformations inherent in all men.

In this last chapter, there are summaries of further techniques of group interaction possible in a modern redevelopment of the Male Mysteries. The foundation of this is, once again, found within the Four Branches. There are many transformative and therapeutic potentials in our simple structure of Companions, Goddesses, and Gods, working through methods of polarity and exchange of energies and ideas according to the basic patterns shown in the Mysteries—patterns which you, the reader, should by now have experienced to a greater or lesser extent by working with the visualizations in this book.

Working with human male companions

For basic experiential group work, I would suggest that a group has no more than five members initially, but that after it has built some trust and companionship, this can be expanded by adding members until it becomes clearly too large to operate efficiently. The group then divides into further groups of five, and so forth. There are no leaders, teachers, or guides, other than those inner guides encountered through your increasing skill in practicing the Mysteries. So to begin, we simply need five men who have already worked individually with the visionary interactions, at least as far as the sequence of the Four Companions, and preferably through the entire cycle of Companions, Goddesses, and Gods, at least once.

As a group, you will recognize a general affinity to a particular Branch within each of you: this is usually a fast and intuitive recognition. Intellectual argument or analytical dissection of character will only waste your time and energy. Besides, everyone in the group takes it in turns to work as a representative of each Branch, so no one is rigidly defined. We all have within us the Warrior, the Poet, the Prophet, the Priest, and the King. Some come to the fore during certain periods of a lifetime; others seem prominent in terms of established persona or character. Sometimes inner work will radically change us, so that a hitherto unconsidered Branch of the male energy and consciousness replaces our conditioned or self-deluded personality and its apparent link to a Branch or archetype.

Foundations of the simple group method

The group method begins by choosing the Four Companions and one Worker. Once this basic choice has been made, the men simply rotate around the cycle, until you have all been a Worker, Warrior, Poet, Prophet, Priest, and of course King.

As a general rule, the group will arrange itself in the fourfold pattern of the Companions. The simple way to do this is to have a chair in each corner of your working room or space (not squarely in the Four Directions, but in the angles the square). The positions are shown in Figure 8.

The worker or primal man sits, initially, at one end of the room, and all five Companions meditate and build the image of the Room with Four Doors, each door being behind or around, and framing, the man chosen during that particular session. This should be a very simple group working, with no long period of time or great effort involved.

The entire sequence of encountering the Branches one by one, and pair by pair, as described in Chapter 10, is then commenced.

But now we encounter a male companion and trusted fellow worker, who mediates or represents the forces of the inner-world contact or archetype. The parts may be read aloud by each man on behalf of his own Branch, or may be worked from an audio recording. When you reach the later stages you do not, of course, literally throw each other through the wall, as in the visualization! Perhaps a large paper hoop could be used, but imagination is far more liberal than manifestation. If you have ever seen any ritual dancing in which a man is raised upon a platform of hands or swords, such ceremonies, found in many cultures, are remnants, preserved in folklore, of the old Male Mysteries. The one who is raised is both King and Worker, exalted and sacrificed. The modern counterpart is the visionary experience whereby you pass through the mirror into the Second Room.

Simply working with the companions in turn, with a group of five men, will occupy a long cycle of experiences. There should be ample opportunities for discussion, noting reactions in all present, and comparing, eventually, how you emerge from the cycle to how you felt when you commenced it. There must also be Silence: any working group must spend periods of time in Silence, as this nourishes everything undertaken. When all five men have worked through the entire cycle, then is the time to form new groups of five, or to bring other men into the initial group.

In conclusion

The foregoing methods are the merest indication of how we might proceed with group work and dramatic or ceremonial pattern making for men. A physical group has an amplifying effect upon some of the subtle energies aroused in the visualizations, but I would stress that the key to balancing this is always by working with the goddess-images, either as a group or individually.

The Male Mysteries are not lost or forgotten. If you steadily work with the content offered in this book, you will come ever closer and more deeply into a syncretic spiritual tradition of transformation. Not ultimately about self, but about relationship and interaction with others. This can only occur when we lose self, and begin to find Self.

If you have read this book all the way through, and practiced the visionary meditative and ritual work described, you are well on your way into the Male Mysteries. Welcome!

APPENDIX 1

Approaching Silence

There are a number of techniques for approaching and entering Silence, used in both Eastern and Western spiritual disciplines or inner training. We shall concentrate upon one closely associated with Western arts of transforming consciousness, as used throughout this book. The method is simple, and is based upon the concept of universal and individual spheres or fields of consciousness/energy/entity, and the Directions of East or Before, South or Right, West or Behind, North or Left, Above and Below. Your center of being is the Seventh Direction, which is Within.

1. Sit in a relaxed upright position (upon a chair or upon the floor if you prefer). For this exercise, the hands are usually laid in the lap, palm up, with the thumb-tips touching ... some experiments will find a comfortable balanced location for the hands using this finger position, either with the back of the left hand over the right, or vice versa. The feet may be lightly crossed at the ankles: again, right over left or left over right is found through your own intuition and preference, as it varies from individual to individual. If you adopt a floor sitting posture, the hand position remains the same, but the legs are usually crossed in the meditator's or hunter's posture, known around

the world since ancient times. Complex yoga postures are not necessary, and should not be taken out of their proper spiritual and cultural context.
2. After a period of steady calming breathing, with eyes closed, a brief vision and definition of the Six Directions is made, as described in our earlier pages. This results in a generally attuned or orientated sphere or field of entity and energy: our self-located within the room, the land, the planet, the universe, aligned according to the Directions and as balanced as possible.
3. We now seek to still customary inner activity (having already stilled outer activity). This is undertaken by inwardly reducing your sense of Time, Space, and Energy, or Movement.

   (a) Seek to suspend your involvement and sense of the passage of Time.
   (b) Seek to suspend your interaction with and sense of Space.
   (c) Seek to still all Energies within and around you, letting go of the urge to Move.

This technique acts upon your entire entity, and makes no separation between inner and outer conditions. The usual method is one of drawing inwards ... as time is stilled, as space is withdrawn, and as energy ceases to interact, we pass deeper and deeper within toward our Source of Being. All that remains is your quiet steady breathing, the breath of life itself.
4. Emerging from Silence involves drawing in a deep breath and exhaling it. This First Breath of air may then be uttered as Four Vowels, realigning the stilled sphere of being. We may, if we choose, go no further than drawing the breath and returning to outer consciousness.

With practice it is possible to reach rapidly through the Three Phases of Timelessness, Spacelessness, and Poise (stilled but ready energy). To begin with, the Approach to Silence requires patience and repeated simple practice. Strenuous effort will produce the opposite results to those required, and trick the mind into many side alleys of trivial interaction.

The secret is to approach the Stillness, the Silence, that is already within us, deep at the center of our being. That Silence is the state of un-being upon which our being is founded. One effective method is to feel for Stillness, the Source of Being, deep within your body, mid-point. Do not identify this Still point with any organ, energy center, or "chakra". It is none of these. Once cross-identifications are cleared, we can begin to seek and find Stillness Within. Within the body, not in the mind. Many people seek Stillness somewhere inside the skull, as if the brain was the sole organ of consciousness. By looking for a metaphysical source, in the center of the body, we progressively undo the idea that consciousness is solely within the skull. In this, ancient tradition and modern research agree ... the entire body is conscious in many ways still unknown to science.

The Approach to Silence creates relative conditions of stillness, peace, and poise. If we truly reached Silence we would pass into a state of existence that cannot be apprehended, for we would reach universal poise, perfect stillness. This condition, if such a word may be used, is found in various definitions in the world's mystical and religious teachings. In our present context, however, we merely seek to Approach Silence, and place no mystical or religious system upon this basic technique of realignment.

APPENDIX 2

Establishing an inner-world contact

This exercise may be undertaken regularly with increasing effect. No specific contact is named in our example, and the method may be used to clarify a number of contacts; with practice it leads to deep and powerful levels of exchange and communication. Focused visualization is educational, in the true sense of the word, leading our consciousness out of its habitual grooves and fixations. Contacts developed through the imagination are invaluable to our general progress toward balance, regardless of any debate over the reality of the entities contacted (see Chapter 3).

A secret method

While visualization is often thought of as an interior process, with the images happening inside the skull, perhaps behind the forehead, there is a key to powerful visions, that was once taught as a secret method. As an example, we can use our vision of the Room described previously. Do not envision the Room inside your head, behind your forehead, in the skull, or anywhere in the interior of your mind. Instead, the imagery is envisioned outside your body. A basic method, called See, Sense, and Feel, is to See the image (the Room in this example) at arm's length or further before you. The image is built by beginning with sight, then Sensing the potential presence to be physical, and finally by Feeling its inherent qualities and attributes. With practice, Seeing, Sensing, and Feeling are simultaneous, though in early training they can be separated.

If the visionary process requires being within the chosen scenario (the Room), the seer moves slowly into the vision after building it. Thus the vision is imagined not as within us, rather we are within the vision.

Computer simulations, as in entertainment and immersive games using virtual reality technology should be avoided if you wish to get strong results from this method. As described previously, virtual reality is something that imposes digital content that is pre-designed. Therefore it impresses upon the imagination an exterior form that is not generated within your consciousness. As this medium becomes increasingly sophisticated, it progressively replaces the living imagination. In the context of Male Mysteries, it is an emasculation.

1. Preparation
Sitting in the center of your Circle, which is either a room, dedicated space, or your own body upon the chair, enter into vision. This is done by closing your eyes and imagining the pictures described, building them slowly and steadily. In guided vision, a script is read, recited or played back from a pre-recorded source.

2. The visualization
Before you is a door (not inside your skull, but before you at arm's length or further); it is a plain wooden door set in a high stone wall. You look upon this door in the wall for some time until it is utterly clear and solid; as you look, you know that the instruction which you seek lies somewhere beyond the entrance that is sealed by the wooden door.

As you look, you sense that the door will not simply open on demand, but only for someone with a valid reason for entry. You meditate upon your reason, clearly defining it in your awareness. In doing so, you inwardly recite a formula for passing through the entrance: "I seek an inner-world contact to teach me the subject of ..." [a chosen subject is focused upon here]. "I seek to pass within under the Light." As you formulate this phrase, you envision a small lamp hanging over the door, with its flame glowing steadily. The door opens, and in vision you rise and pass through the entrance. [This visionary movement can be assisted by the physical movement of a few steps. A typical method requires two chairs, a few feet away from one another, and facing one another. Thus for the return phase, you walk back to your first chair to come out of the vision]. You may also work through the entire process standing or sitting, without ritual movement.

Envision [see Sense and Feel] that you are in a small courtyard; it is square, surrounded by high stone walls. In the center is a fountain bubbling from a circular basin. The courtyard floor is of flagstones, inscribed with faint designs. Against each of the four walls, there grows a flowering tree, and below the branches of each tree, just to one side of the trunk, there is a door in each wall.

You walk into the center of the courtyard, and move from left to right around the fountain, remembering your stated purpose for being admitted. You are waiting for a teacher or adviser to appear through one of the Four Doors where the blossoms fall. As you pace around the stone basin with its gentle trickle of water, you hear a door open and close quietly behind you. You turn, and place your hands upon the edge of the basin of the fountain. Standing opposite you is your teacher.

At this point, the effect of the vision will vary. Some people cannot see their inner-world contact immediately, and although the door always opens the contact sometimes remains out of sight, speaking, or communicating wordlessly, while you continue to walk slowly around the fountain. Others may see their teacher immediately. It is very important to remember, and write down at a later time of recollection, the appearance of the contact; his or her face, clothing, any identifying objects or symbols, any suggestions of a name. Sometimes such details take a long time in coming forth; some contacts are reliable for years before you see an image or know a name. There is no need to try and force a contact to give you a name, providing you have a mode or symbol of identification.

The identification is often established through your body. How did the body feel when the inner-world teacher became present? In subsequent workings, let your body remember for you.

There is no further guided part to this working, other than the simple closing pattern, which is described below. For obvious reasons, the subject matter of the interaction between yourself and an inner-world being will vary infinitely, and only a general summary can be given regarding what might reasonably occur.

After re-stating the subject matter chosen for education or enlightenment (though this is often unnecessary) you conduct a conversation, an exchange, with the contact. This is actually a type of mediation, as distinct from meditation, combined with images; in advanced stages, the imagery fades into a more direct knowledge transfer of the subject in hand.

In the initial stages, the subject matter should be carefully restricted and the time period kept short. Once you are attuned to a contact, a series of further inner experiences may be undertaken; the teacher may lead the student through a door, or present specific scenarios through the imagination. The student, however, should not merely wander about willy-nilly, but keep to the matter in hand. If the contact is within established spiritual traditions, there will be little or no idle wandering allowed, and a drifting consciousness on the part of the seeker/student will either break the contact or result in a reminder of the function and purpose of the meeting.

If in doubt about time duration, set an arbitrary period of comfortable length, say 15 or 20 minutes, before starting the visualization. Our inner clock will usually begin to withdraw the awareness at the time indicated ... never use any mechanical or electronic means of interruption. The question of duration is subjective, and soon becomes a matter of individual or group style. A summary of the subject matter should be written out as soon as possible after withdrawing from the inner place, though experienced mediators may do so while retaining the inner contact in the imagination.

3. Closing the contact

Now the communication is over, you are standing back in the courtyard, with your hands resting upon the bowl of the fountain. A door closes quietly behind you, and you Sense and Feel that your inner-world contact has departed. You begin to walk slowly from left to right around the square courtyard; suddenly, you feel prompted to stop in front of one of the flowering trees; you know intuitively that the door by this tree is the one that leads to your own outer world. There may be a symbol or object hanging from the lower-most branches; if there is, remember it, for it is a key to further experience in the inner-world, a key which may be used to pass to and fro easily. The door opens, and you adjust your senses to relate once more to your room and chair beyond. You pass through, and hear the door close behind you. Slowly you merge back into the image of yourself seated in a room, facing the stone wall and the closed door. The image of the wall dissolves, and you open your eyes. All that remains is to close the Circle according to your custom.

4. Conclusion

Write out your experience; wait for at least a week, then write a commentary upon the experience. This last is a very useful method, as much will come that is not clear in the initial description.

APPENDIX 3

Visualization: the Guardian

In this expanded narrative, we seek to establish contact with one of the great primal god-forms, central to the Male Mysteries, and widely found in ancient Mysteries, magical arts, and religion. We should always be aware that a working image or method within an apparently outmoded ancient religion or formal tradition does not preclude its modern use. The mythic roots of each god- and goddess-form, or specific methods of transforming awareness, are far deeper than any formal presentation or cultural expression.

When we use images of this type to regenerate our inner energies, we are tapping into the mythic roots rather than any specific cult or historical or religious flowering of those roots. We are, in fact, slowly building a new Branch of the Mysteries for the coming century. The image of the Guardian is known worldwide in many variants, each variant having a fundamental identity and similar appearance to an archetypical Guardian. Local and historical expressions can and do take on specific forms and functions, and we need to be aware of the differences; indeed, the differences between expressions of an archetypical god- or goddess-form, ranging from universal to purely local, are important in direct work with images and energies.

There is a constant emphasis in modern spiritual or meditative teaching that we must assert the unity and uniformity of all such images and traditions, that they are all ultimately one. This may be true, but for us as humans the way begins with a clear understanding of one or two specific paths. These paths ultimately lead to unity, but we must travel the path first, and cannot reach unity by merely acknowledging it intellectually.

When we talk of the Guardian, this is not simply an outmoded or redundant ancient god-form, but an enduring image inherent within human consciousness, an image that leads to the presence of a living god-form. For practical purposes, it gives shape and entity as a living being to certain male forces or energies, which we all, male and female, have within us. These energies, however, are not confined to any one male, single human, imaginative or transpersonal entity, or to a transformation of the psyche; they are also found in the environment, the land, the planet, the Cosmos.

There is an individual or microcosmic reflection of any god-form, and a transpersonal or macrocosmic image. The greater image is not simply some type of vaguely universal god or goddess-form, for it has an extremely potent and enduring presence within the collective consciousness of many life forms, not just humans. As far as we are concerned, this is essentially our collective ancestral consciousness, a realm of consciousness that is frequently used to great effect in the esoteric traditions of transformation and empowerment.

The forces embodied by the Guardian are also embodied by certain goddesses, but the gender of the image alters and defines the manner in which it works, and attunes its deep effect upon human beings.

In the Classical world, the Guardian god was known as Pan, the lord of nature, of the wild forces of growth, the creative energies that flow through all forms within the land. The wild energies of this god were said to be impossible to resist: his presence brought the fit of panic that is felt when potent energies are at work.

Modern fiction, based upon religious propaganda, has tended to brand this image as evil, licentious, savage, degenerate. The early Church fathers identified Pan as a false god, *deo falsus*, eventually to be conflated with the Middle-Eastern *shaitan*, Satan, or the Devil. The sanctity of nature was regarded with suspicion by the Church. Nature was seen as a delusion or as a source of evil and temptation. The elect were supposed to be uplifted to heaven as rapidly as possible, leaving the damned to burn in hell, and ignoring an abandoned Earth far behind. Surprisingly, perhaps, this dualistic escapist elitism reappears, in subtle variants, in much of the current fashionable New Age literature and related teachings. To emphasize light against or over darkness is one of the more enervating concepts that limits spiritual understanding and development; light and darkness exist in a rhythm together, and humans, like plants and simpler life forms, require the cycle of light and darkness to grow and change. Excessive light or darkness, periods of either that are too long or too short, lead to imbalance. If we extend this analogy or resonance to plant growth a little further, we might liken the Mysteries and the perennial techniques of transformation to a deep understanding and practical application of the secret rhythms of nature.

On an inner level, the god Pan represents not only wild vital forces, but the Herdsman or controller of such forces. It is through his power that we both grow and learn to give form to growth, to drive and harmonize our energies according to a set of natural simple laws. Thus he is also a god of taking, of limitation. The Mysteries of Pan, or of his Celtic counterpart Cernunnos, to whom we shall turn shortly, were particularly loathed by the orthodox Churches, as they represented a way of spiritual liberation through natural energies, and were closely linked to an ancient pervasive worship of the Great Mother. The Herdsman, Guardian, or Green Man is the wild son of the Great Mother. The Horned God, known to the Celts as Cernunnos, was widespread in the ancient world; versions of his image are found in prehistoric cave paintings, and as far West as the Americas among the gods of the native people. He is Guardian of the Mysteries of the Underworld, sometimes shown (as in Romano-Celtic images from the 1st century BCE) sitting upon or close to a hoard of coins, gold, or precious metalwork. He holds serpents in either hand, and was often identified with the fruits of the Earth, both in the form of animals and growing plants. One of the most famous representations of this god is found in the silver Gündestrup Cauldron, dating from the 2nd century BCE. The narrative sequence of pictures upon the cauldron are typical of the Male Mysteries and their relationship to the great Mystery of life, death, and rebirth.

Thus we might summarize this deity, embodying a set or pattern of energies, as the Keeper, the Protector, and the refiner of forces into beneficial form. No beneficial growth or form can occur without limitation, purification, and selection. So the Guardian is also a god of taking, of challenge. In human terms, he is the Guardian of thresholds of consciousness and energy: he prevents us from accessing more energy than we may safely cope with, yet if we are able to pass through his strict tests, controls and therapeutic inner transformations, he gives us free entry to realms of subtle powers and spiritual transformation.

Other guardians arise within consciousness due to individual circumstances, and are known upon collective levels; some are found only in sacred locations. But as far as humanity is concerned, the Guardian is generally the pervasive image of a horned man. While awareness of this image and its potential has been suppressed in our culture for several centuries, it returns now, inevitably, as we awaken to the destruction and pollution of nature ... by which we include ourselves as both aggressors and victims of such madness and irresponsibility. The Guardian was, and is, one of the major controls of such madness, leading the wild energies into proper paths. Due to our removal of this image, and related goddess-images, from our lives, we have run riot over the land, the oceans, the planet. The terrible results are now becoming only too clear, the results of excessive forced growth in artificial light, with no recuperative empowering darkness.

Men can be not only Warriors for the World, but Guardians of Growth.

Meeting the Guardian

The individual or group spends a preparatory period in silence, using the meditation of Stillness, a calming, clearing technique. As always with such preparatory stages, the emphasis must be upon stillness and silence, and not on any specific image, divine or meditative form, or religious meditational technique. The aim of this period of stillness is to calm all energies/thoughts/emotions and so become ready for a clear, unconfused or undistracted image to be built and to work within the imagination. The envisioning, always outside the skull, is as follows:

First, we envision a forest: tall trees and primal untouched woodland growth. The great trees rise up to the sunlit sky above, filtering the light through their huge canopy of branches, until it falls in green and golden shafts and pools upon the rich carpet of deep loam and mosses below. This is an ancient oak forest, and many of the trees have wide gnarled trunks showing great age.

Gradually we enter into this forest, and feel the presence of the trees, emanating an intense radiant force, a subtle warmth and vibrancy all around us. We hear birds calling as the wind constantly stirs the leaves and higher branches, making a ceaseless flowing sound like the rippling of water, the tides of the sea. As we walk deeper into the forest, we find a narrow deer trail, and follow this through the trees to a clearing. The clearing is small, with a huge ancient wide trunked oak tree in the center, growing out of a pile of massive tumbled rocks.

From a cleft in the rocks, a tiny spring flows, making a damp pool of lush green growth. We see that the rocks are red, and that there are tracks of many animals coming to this central spring, to drink the water, and lick the mineral salts. In this clearing we pause, and wait in silence, affirming that we seek the presence of the Guardian. [Here a silent pause is made in the narrative or guided vision. The length of time depends upon the individual or group. For individual work, this is usually a brief period, but for guided work with groups it may be lengthened.]

As we meditate, we Sense, See, and Feel that we have been joined by someone. From behind the tree, a man has emerged, who looks steadily upon us in calm, unhurried judgment. He is a teacher and guide in the Male Mysteries, and is willing to take us into the presence of the Guardian if we truly seek to do so. With this man, there is an animal, keeping him close company. Look upon the animal and remember it.

Our guide beckons us toward the spring rising from the rocks, and shows us a small scarred rough stone bowl by the side of the water. He fills this with water and splashes some water into our faces, in lustration and preparation. The water is ice-cold and shocks us wide-awake. Even as we wipe the water from our eyes, we see that our guide has moved behind the tree, and we hurry to follow him.

As we pass to the other side of the tree, we seem to step from light to darkness, day to night. Ahead of us we see the guide and his animal passing swiftly over a bare star-lit plain; the trees of the forest have disappeared, and the ground is hard and cold. We are running now, and we must breathe deeply to keep up with our guide and his companion animal. The cold air fills our lungs as we breath in and out, gaining speed with every breath. The effort is hard at first, but gradually brings with it a deep rhythm that gives us increasing strength.

Far ahead, we see a glimmer of light, as if the sun is beginning to rise: as we settle into the rhythm of running and breathing, we See, Sense, and Feel that the plain is not empty, as we had first thought. Occasionally on either side, we see the dim shapes of other creatures moving in the starlight. Sometimes they approach, as if curious, while others flee at our coming. Some of the shapes are vast, and we uneasily sense creatures from other times and places, creatures which we might fear. Yet the speed and rhythm of our running moves us swiftly ahead, following our guide and his animal: their presence seems to deter anything from being too curious or coming too close.

In the growing dawn light, we come to the end of the bare plain. Our guide slows his pace and pauses to wait for us to approach. We find that we are once again on the edge of a forest, and as the sun rises a dawn chorus begins, many birds call to the light. This forest is of trees and plants that we have never seen: the trees have a smooth glossy green and red bark, rising to a vast height, and the leaves far above shed a deep blue and purple light, filtering the sun as it rises. The crying birds lift a vast chorus of calls and whistles, which is joined by the roaring of great beasts, and the shrilling of small animals in the huge branches above. As we ran across the plain, we felt like warriors at the chase, but now we feel small, like children, dwarfed by the tall trees, and the presence of such seething, roaring life.

Our guide briefly touches the animal that accompanies him, and they step aside to reveal an entrance leading into the Earth at the foot of two huge trees. The thick smooth roots of these trees tangle together, forming a low arch, and our guide indicates that we must pass within. We feel the growing heat and light of the day, and the air is moist and filled with powerful scents. Within those shadowy roots seems to be a resting place, a shelter embraced by the primal forest, and we slowly stoop to pass within.

We find ourselves in a low earthen passageway, which leads gently downwards. It is of hard compacted soil, and bears the marks of many passing claws; suddenly, we are less certain about this place. Our guide and his companion animal have remained above, and we move slowly downwards alone. The tunnel widens out into a large chamber, which has a strong animal smell for many beasts have sheltered here. The far of end of this chamber is lit by tiny lamps burning with a dim yellow flame: a raised platform of fresh green branches is laid there, and we smell strong resins and sharp bitter herbs, cutting through the primal odor. As we look upon this platform, we feel a deep fear rise within us, making our hair stand on end, and our skin shiver. We know that we are in the presence of the Guardian, and his power brings us to the edge of panic.

Set far back in the shadows, where the light of the lamps barely touches, we See, Sense, and Feel that a figure is sitting cross-legged upon the green branches. His face is hidden from us, but we see strong sinewy arms and legs, covered in deep spiraling tattoos. The flickering lamplight first reveals and then conceals these patterns, which seem to writhe like snakes upon his dark skin. We see that he has long hair and a beard, and that a tall crown of spreading antlers is upon his head. His eyes are in shadow, and we are, for the moment, relieved that he does not look fully upon us in the light. Slowly, uncertainly, we sit, and gradually calm ourselves, waiting in the presence of the Guardian. [Here there is a silent period: this should be as long as possible].

As we sit we gain many insights concerning the Guardian: what he conceals, what he reveals, how he may keep us from passing where we might destroy ourselves, and how he may prevent us from destroying that which we do not understand. In the lamplight his face is slowly revealed to those that dare to look upon him. He sits still, unmoving, unmoved by our presence, yet we feel a huge vigor and power flowing out from him; it encompasses us, enters into us, and triggers energies within our selves that we have not known before. [A brief silence here.]

As we sit in that underground chamber, we slowly discover that the scent in the warm air is changing. At first, it was the odor of many animals, merging with that of the Earth itself. Next was the resinous and sharp smell of herbs and healing plants rising from the leafy platform at the end of the chamber; now, this astringent smell is replaced by that of flowers. Faint at first, then with increasing presence, we smell the perfume of many different flowers, as if the blooms from a rich wild garden in a fertile land have been scattered all around us.

As this complex and delicate sequence of perfumes grows stronger, we see that another figure is standing at the edge of the raised platform. In the lamplight, we see that this is a beautiful young woman with long flowing hair; she wears a simple robe woven with a pattern of plants and flowers. The figure of the Guardian has receded into deepest shadow, though we know that he remains seated on the platform. The lamplight reflects from the brilliant color of the young woman's dress, revealing first one plant, then another, then scenes and images, woven in and out of the flowers, hidden deep within the pattern of the fabric.

We look upon her long hair and shining eyes; her presence lifts many shadows from our hearts, our personal shadows that the Guardian had drawn up from deep within us. The young woman steps across the chamber, and as she moves the perfume of flowers grows intense; the sound of her robe is like the rustling of a great garden in the early morning wind. At the entranceway, she lifts her hand, and we see that she holds a small living branch, with roots, fresh green leaves, buds, opening flowers. We pause to look upon her standing at the doorway. [Here a short silent pause is made.]

Now, this goddess beckons to us, and we follow her through the tunnel and up the sloping way toward the surface. We emerge into red sunlight, shining directly into our eyes, making them water. Even as we recover our sight, we discover that she has vanished, and that we stand back at the original clearing in the first oak forest, in the light of sunset. We have emerged where we began, coming from a passageway concealed within the roots of the oak tree, out through the rocks that release the tiny spring into the glade. In the trees, we can see the movement of many animals, making their way through the woods, and we hear the evening song of birds. The forest is filled with a sense of restfulness and peace. [Here, a brief pause is made.]

We sense that our guide and his companion animal wait at the edge of the glade, and know that we must travel with them down the narrow deer trail through the trees. As they lead us out of the forest, the sun sets, casting long shadows through the trees. At the very forest edge, our guide bids us sit and rest. Once again, that profound sense of peace that permeates the land at sunset washes through us, and we close our eyes to sit in silence at the threshold of day and night. [Take a short pause here; you might fall asleep for a while.]

Gradually the sounds and scents of the oak forest fade away, and we quietly return to our outer world: in our inner vision the trees dissolve, and we feel the springy grass beneath us become the surface of a chair. We slowly open our eyes, and return to a familiar room.

Our meeting with the Guardian and the Maiden is over. [Notes may be made at this point, or a discussion if required. It is important that people are not forced in any way to share their experiences, and no demands should be made upon anyone unwilling to describe their experiences.]

BIBLIOGRAPHY

1. Versluis, Arthur. *Entering the Mysteries: The Secret Traditions of Indigenous Europe*, ISBN 13 9781596500228
2. Johnson, K. Paul. *The Masters Revealed: Madame Blavatsky and the Myth of the Great White Lodge*, ISBN 9780791420645
3. Graves, R. *The White Goddess*, Faber and Faber, London, 1975
   The Greek Myths, Penguin, Harmondsworth (2 vols) 1965
   Breton Connelly, Joan. *The Parthenon Enigma*, ISBN 9780307476593
   Portrait of a Priestess, ISBN 9780691127460
   Aisler, Riane. *The Chalice and The Blade: Our History, Our Future.* ISBN 13 9780062502896
4. Sjöo, & Mor, B. *The Great Cosmic Mother*, Harper and Row, San Francisco, 1987
   Ruth Barrett (ed) *Female Erasure: What You Need to Know About Gender Politics War on Women, the Female Sex and Human Rights.* Tidal Time Publishing, London, 2018
   Stone, M. *When God was a Woman*, Dial Press, London, 1976
5. Jung, C.G. *Archetypes of the Collective Unconsciousness* and *The Concept of the Collective Unconscious* in *Collected Works, Vol. 9, Part 1*, Princeton University Press, Princeton, 1968
   Man and His Symbols, Aldus, London, 1979

Wilhelm, R. and Jung, C.G. *The Secret of the Golden Flower*, Routledge Kegan Paul, London, 1972
Moussaieff Masson, J. *Against Therapy: Emotional Tyranny and the Myth of Psychological Healing* ISBN 978-1567510225
Noll, Richard. *The Jung Cult: Origins of a Charismatic Movement*, ISBN 9780691037240
The Aryan Christ: The Secret Life of Carl Jung, ISBN 978-0679449454
6. https://en.wikipedia.org/wiki/Climate_emergency_declaration
7. ibid. Sjöo, note (4) above
8. Fortune, Dion. *The Sea Priestess*, London 1938 and subsequent editions
9. Mookerjee, Ajit. *Kali: The Feminine Force*, ISBN 9780892812127
The Tantric Way: Art, Science, Ritual, ISBN 9780500270882
10. ibid. Johnson, K. Paul, note (2) above
11. Tolstoy, N. *The Quest for Merlin*, Hamish Hamilton, London, 1985
Stewart, R.J. *Merlin: The Prophetic Vision and Mystic Life*, Routledge, London, 1995
12. https://en.wikipedia.org/wiki/Hillel_the_Elder
13. Walsh Z. *A Meta-Critique of Mindfulness Critiques: From McMindfulness to Critical Mindfulness*. In: Purser R., Forbes D., Burke A. (eds) *Handbook of Mindfulness. Mindfulness in Behavioral Health*. Springer, Cham, https://doi.org/10.1007/978-3-319-44019-4_11
14. Froma I. Zeitlin (Ed), John J. Winkler (Ed), and David M. Halperin (Ed). *Before Sexuality: The Construction of Erotic Experience in the Ancient Greek World*, ISBN 9780691002217
15. Stewart, R.J. *The Merlin Tarot*, Aquarian Press, Wellingborough, 1988 and subsequent editions
16. Plato. *Republic, the Myth of Er* (vision of *Ananke and the Three Fates*) various editions
17. Yates, Frances. *The Art of Memory*, London, 1966
18. Stewart, R.J. *Living Magical Arts*, Blandford, 1990
19. Stewart, R.J. *The Sphere of Art, vol I*, 2008, ISBN 9780979140266 Assembling and working with the Sphere. (& CD) *The Sphere of Art vol II*, 2012, ISBN 9780981924694; *Aesch Mezareph: the Purifying Fire. Qabalistic Alchemy and Transformation*. The Sphere of Art vol III, ISBN 9780985600648
20. Stewart R.J. *Elements of Prophecy*. Shaftesbury, 1991
21. Matthews, J. (ed). *At the Table of the Grail*. ISBN 13 9781842930359
22. Stewart, R.J. *Cuchullainn, Hound of Ulster*. ISBN 9781853140037
23. Stewart, R.J. *The Miracle Tree, Demystifying the Qabalah*. ISBN 9781564146502
24. ibid note (15) above
25. ibid note (18) above
26. ibid note (23) above
27. Stewart, R.J. *Where is St George?* ISBN 0239001699
28. ibid note (11) above

FURTHER READING

Angus, S. *The Mystery Religions and Christianity*, John Murray, London, 1925.
Berendt, Joachim-Ernst. *The Third Ear*, Element Books, Shaftesbury 1987.
Bolen, J.S. *Gods in Everyman*, Harper and Row, San Francisco, 1989.
Cumont, F. *Oriental Religions in Roman Paganism*, Dover, New York, 1955.
Eliade, M. *From Primitives to Zen*, Collins, London 1977.
King, William (1710) *An Historical Account of the Heathen Gods and Heroes*, reprinted with introduction by Ross Nichols, Centaur Press, London, 1965.
Lustig, Robert H. *The Hacking of the American Mind: The Science Behind the Corporate Takeover of Our Bodies and Brains*, ISBN 9781101982945MacCana, P. *Celtic Mythology*, Hamlyn, London, 1975.
Matthews, C. *Arthur and the Sovereignty of Britain*, Penguin, Arkana, London, 1987.
Matthews, J. (ed) *The Choirs of the God*, Unwin Hyman, London, 1991.
Oesterly, W.O.E. & Robinson, T.H. *Hebrew Religion, Its Origin and Development*, SPCK, London, 1940.
Steinbrecher, E. *The Inner Guide Meditation*, Aquarian Press, Wellingborough, 1988.
Wind, E. *Pagan Mysteries in the Renaissance*, Oxford University Press, Oxford 1980.

FURTHER READING

INDEX

all-male Master, 40. *See also* teachers and pupils
ancestors and mentors, 63
ancestral contact, 92–93, 136
ancestral Ireland, 79
ancient visions, 105–106. *See also* visualizing transformation
antagonistic dualism, xxiv
"appearing as male figures", 35. *See also* teachers and pupils
archangel, 118
archetypes, 4, 115
　psychological, 4
atrophies, imagination, 104–105
Autolycus, xxx
awakening awareness, 61

balanced humanity, 23. *See also* men and the goddess
basic experiential group work, 154
Below, 86

Besant, A., xxi
Bright One, 59

caste systems, 60
Cernunnos, 116, 169–170. *See also* Guardian
chakras, 124
Christianity, 90
　in magical arts, 118
　failure of Christianity, 16
Classical
　goddesses, 75
　god-forms, 13
　Greek, xxv
collective
　tradition of initiation, 62
　unconscious, 92–93
concentrated image-making, 105. *See also* visualizing transformation
conscious visualization, 103–105. *See also* visualizing transformation

INDEX

crude and cruel teaching methods, xxvii
cults and movements, 39
cultural stream of contact, 136

dancer, 65. *See also* warrior
Dark God, 116
Dark Mother, 116
darkness, xxiv
Dark Son, 116
deep memory, 110
"demon Jehovah", 15
Direction Above, 85–86
Divine, 67. *See also* King within; prophet
    Being, 4
    Kings, 87
Doors and Mirror, 129. *See also* Room with Four Doors
dualism, antagonistic, xxiv

East, 84
Eastern religions, 40–41
educational initiatory traditions, 3
elder, wise, xxviii–xxix
empowerment and transformation, 123
    ancestral stream of contact, 136
    detailed work program, 123
    development through imagination, 125
    encountering Five Branches, 130, 132–133
    encountering poet, 133–134
    encountering priest, 135
    encountering prophet, 134
    encountering the gods, 149–152
    energy centers, 124
    Five Branches pattern, 123
    Four Goddesses, 140–141
    Four Gods, 144–149
    Goddess of Inspiration and Intuition, 142
    Goddess of the Land, 143
    Great Goddess of all Being, 143–144
    inner contacts or people, 135–137
    lunar cycle of energies, 124
    lunar timing, 140
    Pentagonal Room, 131
    Room with Four Doors, 125–127, 129–130
    short time scale, 139–140
    sleeping and wounded king, 138–139
    sleeping king, 137
    Three Thresholds, 125, 138
    visions and encounters, 137–138
    using visualization for, 123–124
    Warrior Goddess, 141–142
    12-week cycle, 137
    12-week working timetable, 139
energy, 12, 99. *See also* men and the goddess
    centers, 124
    exchange of, 100
    -exchanging bodies, 24
    lunar cycle of, 124
    psychic, 115
    sexual, 106
English Saint George, 119–120
"enlightenment", xxi
envisioning future, 100–103. *See also* visualizing transformation
esoteric
    methods of self transformation, 98
    tradition, 7, 101
exercises, 97. *See also* visualizing transformation
experiential group work, basic, 154

false hero, 76. *See also* warrior
female entity, 6
feminine counterparts, 43. *See also* polarity and sexuality
Five Branches, 55–56, 79
    ancestors and mentors, 63
    awakening awareness and bringing inner change, 61
    Bright One, 59
    caste systems, 60
    collective tradition of initiation, 62
    hero, 77–78

idealized society, 60
images and concepts in general
  magical arts, 61
inner-world teachers, 63
Irish hero Cuchulainn, 77
and male body, 58
masks and vehicles, 59–61
pattern, 57, 123
poet, 65–66, 133–134
priest, 64–65, 135
prophet, 66–69, 134
romantic escapism, 61
Room with Four Doors, 130–133
rule in magical arts, 63
skills and crafts, 61–63
traditional attributes of, 58–59
warrior, 69–71, 130–132
Warrior Departure, 132–133
Western Esoteric Tradition, 61
folk tradition of initiation, 62
fourfold Elemental pattern, 79
Four Goddesses, 140–141
  Goddess of Inspiration and
    Intuition, 142
  Goddess of the Land, 143
  Great Goddess of all Being, 143–144
  Warrior Goddess, 141–142
Four Gods, 144–145
  Above, 149
  Below, 149
  cultural god-forms relating to, 146
  East, 148
  nature of, 145–148
  North, 149
  sacred space, 147–148
  South, 148
  West, 148
future, envisioning, 100–103. *See also*
  visualizing transformation

gender. *See also* god-within/-without;
  men and the goddess
  and polarity, 6–12
  -rigid suppositions, 22–23
  and spirituality, 22
geometry, 82

God. *See also* god-forms; magic gods
  and visions; prophet
  -and goddess-forms, 115
  in human form, 67–68
  men and, 3–5
  psychology and, 4
  three aspects of, 12–15
  and visions, 120
  in Western magical arts, 115
Goddess, 75. *See also* Four Goddesses
  ancient male aggression toward, 75
  Classical, 75
  of Inspiration and Intuition, 142
  of sexuality and death, 75
  of the Land, 143
  -within, 21
god-forms, 115–116. *See also* magic gods
  and visions
  classical, 13
  mirroring of, 118–120
  specific, 68
  upon Tree of Life, 121
gods, 149–152
  encountering the, 149–152
  God of Life-Giving and
    Life-Taking, 150
  god of light and darkness, 151
  God of Perfect Love and
    Immaculate Death, 150
  Gods of the Four Directions,
    151–152
  men and, 3–5
  psychology and the, 4
god-within/-without, 3, 5–6, 21.
  See also god-forms
  abuse of nature, 5
  "demon Jehovah", 15
  energy, 12
  essentials behind magic, religion,
    and myth, 3
  failure of Christianity, 16
  female entity, 6
  finding the god-within, 15–19
  gender and polarity, 6–12
  inward-looking meditation, 17
  long-term effects of dogma, 4

male-dominated New Age
  spirituality, 18
male entity, 6
materialism, 5
Medallion Man, 17
men and the god, 3–5
  monotheism, 13
  Not One Being, 16
  One Being, 13
  perennial educational initiatory
    traditions, 3
  polarity thresholds, 11–12
  psychological archetypes, 4
  psychology and the gods, 4
  rivalry and pain between father
    and son, 15
  three aspects of man or god,
    12–15
  Three Faces, The, 14–15
  Tree of Life, The, 7, 9–10
  Wheel of Life, The, 7–8
Gordian Knot, xxiv–xxv
grail, 72–76
Grail legends, 73, 77
Grail, The, 73
Graves, R., xxiv
Great Goddess, 21. *See also* Four
    Goddesses; men and the
    goddess
  of all Being, 143–144
  of sexuality and death, 75
Green Man. *See* Guardian
group method, simple, 155–156
group work. *See also* visualizing
    transformation
  basic experiential, 154
  with reader or recite, 111
Guardian, 167. *See also* visualization
  Cernunnos, 169–170
  in Classical world, 168
  meeting the Guardian, 170–174
  Pan, 168–169
  variants, 167

Herdsman. *See* Guardian
hero, 76–78. *See also* Five Branches;
  warrior

Hidden Masters, xxiii, 38–41. *See also*
  teachers and pupils
hidden traditions and training, 98
homosexuality, 46–52. *See also* polarity
  and sexuality
human Elemental personae, 80
humanity, balanced, 23. *See also* men
  and the goddess

ideal society, 60, 71–72
image-making, concentrated,
  105. *See also* visualizing
    transformation
imagination, 104. *See also* visualizing
    transformation
  atrophies, 104–105
  development through, 125
  imposition of will, xxviii
  individual power-centers, 99
initiation, collective tradition of, 62
inner
  change, 61
  constructs, 107
  contacts, 135–137
  Inner Fire, 106
inner-world contact, 161
  secret method, 161–165
  See, Sense, and Feel method,
    161–162
  vision of the Room, 161
  visualization, 161
inner-world teachers, 63. *See also*
  teachers and pupils
  identifying, 35–38
  working with, 33–35
Inspiration and Intuition,
  Goddess of, 142
Irish hero Cuchulainn, 77
Irish Morrigan, 75, 77

Jehovah, demon, 15
Jung, C. G., xxx

karma and evolution, xxiii
King, 55. *See also* Five Branches;
  sleeping king
  wounded, 138–139

King Arthur, 71, 77. *See also* warrior
Kingship, 87. *See also* King within
King within, 87
    ancestral contact, 92–93
    Christianity, 90
    collective unconscious, 92–93
    Divine or Sacred Kings, 87
    holisms within holisms, 91
    Kingship, 87
    Melchizedek, 90–91
    Sacred Kingship, 88–93
knightly code, 75. *See also* warrior

label, xxxi
labelling the problem, xxxi–xxxii
Land, Goddess of the, 143
light, xxiv
Light Mother, 116
Light Son, 116
lunar cycle of energies, 124
lunar timing, 140

magic, 107, 113. *See also* magic gods and visions
    of Poet or Bard, 133–134
    science and, 113
    sexual, 24
magical arts. *See also* magic gods and visions
    Christianity in, 118
    god in Western, 115
    images and concepts in, 61
    rule in, 63
    use of images in, 114
magic gods and visions, 113
    archangel, 118
    archetype, 115
    Christianity in magical arts, 118
    Dark God, 116
    Dark Mother, 116
    Dark Son, 116
    English Saint George, 119–120
    essential distinction, 116–117
    god-and goddess-forms, 115
    god-forms, 115–116
    god-forms upon the Tree of Life, 121
    god in Western magical arts, 115
    gods and visions, 120
    Light Mother, 116
    Light Son, 116
    Merlin, 120
    Middle Eastern variants, 118
    mirroring of god-forms, 118–120
    Pan or Cernunnos, 116
    psychic properties or energies, 115
    science and magic, 113
    spiritual or magical tradition, 114
    Tree of Life, 117–118
    universal God, 116
    use of images in magical arts, 114
    visualization of deities, 114
male
    -dominated New Age spirituality, 18
    entity, 6
    and female shape, 83
male figures, appearing as, 35. *See also* teachers and pupils
Male Mysteries, xxvi–xxvii, xxxii
    basic experiential group work, 154
    development through imagination, 125
    empowering techniques, 5
    Five Branches, 55–56
    foundations of simple group method, 155–156
    future of, 153–156
    magnetic men with golden auras, xxvii
    male initiation and transformation, xxvi
    transformative Branches or modes of, 55–56
    working with male companions, 154–155
manipulation of images, 49–50. *See also* polarity and sexuality
Mantle, 33. *See also* teachers and pupils
masks and vehicles, 59–61. *See also* Five Branches

184 INDEX

Masters, the, xxii, 29. *See also* teachers and pupils
    cults and movements, 39
    hidden Masters
    Hidden Masters, xxiii, 38–41
    karma and evolution, xxiii
    New Age Hidden Masters, 41
    spiritual evolution, xxiii–xxiv
    superior male concepts, xxii
    Theosophical Society, 39
materialism, 5
Medallion Man, 17
meditation, 100
Melchizedek, 90–91. *See also* King within
memory, deep, 110
men and the god, 3–5. *See also* god-within/-without
    three aspects of, 12–15
men and the goddess, 21
    balanced humanity, 23
    energy-exchanging bodies, 24
    gender and spirituality, 22
    gender-rigid suppositions, 22–23
    goddess-within, 21
    god-within, 21
    Great Goddess, 21
    mother and lover, 26–27
    perceiving as she, 25–26
    sexual magic, 24
    spiritual balance, 23–24
    stereotypes within revival of Goddess awareness, 26
    Tantra, 24
    transcendence through celibacy, 24–25
    transformation of perception, 25–26
    weaknesses of therapy, 23
mentor, personal, 29–33. *See also* teachers and pupils
mentorship, xxix. *See also* teaching
Merlin, 37, 120
metaphysical teachers, 33–34. *See also* teachers and pupils
mindfulness, 43. *See also* polarity and sexuality

mirroring of god-forms, 118–120. *See also* magic gods and visions
model society, 71–72
monotheism, 13, 68
mother and lover, 26–27. *See also* men and the goddess
Mysteries, xx
    ancient Mysteries of Isis, xxiv
    of ancient world, xx
    imposition of will, xxviii
    male and female, xxvi–xxvii
    Male Mysteries, xxvi
    modern, xxvi–xxvii
    realization of delusion, xxvii
    spirituality and polarity, xxi
    transformations and realizations of, xxvii–xxviii
mystics, 68. *See also* prophet
mythic lore, 105

New Age. *See also* prophet; teachers and pupils
    channeling and spiritual mastery, 69
    Hidden Masters, 41
    movement, 100
non-sentimental manner teaching, xxvii
North, 85
Not One Being, 16

One Being, 13. *See also* god-within/-without

Pan, 116, 168–169. *See also* Guardian
Past Lives, 44. *See also* polarity and sexuality
Pentagonal Room, 131. *See also* Room with Four Doors
perceiving as she, 25–26. *See also* men and the goddess
perception transformation, 25–26. *See also* men and the goddess
perennial educational initiatory traditions, 3

INDEX

Perennial Tradition. *See* Western Esoteric Tradition
personal meditation and concentration, 99
personal teacher/mentor, 29–33. *See also* teachers and pupils
physical use of body, 99
poet, 55, 65, 133–134. *See also* Five Branches
   and bard, 66, 133–134
   music, 65
   transition from warrior or poet to prophet, 69
polarity and sexuality, 43
   feminine counterparts, 43
   homosexuality, 46–52
   manipulation of images, 49–50
   mindfulness, 43
   Past Lives, 44
   sexual initiation, 44–46
   temple sexuality, 44
polarity thresholds, 11–12
politically influential magical Orders, xxii
power-centers, individual, 99
pre-recorded audio, 110–111. *See also* visualizing transformation
Presence of the Inner Warrior, 132
priest, 55, 64, 135. *See also* Five Branches
   genetic tendency, 64–65
   priesthood, 64
primal heroes, 76. *See also* warrior
primal universal patterns, 82
prophet, 55, 66, 134. *See also* Five Branches
   monotheism, 68
   mystics and visionaries, 68
   New Age channeling and spiritual mastery, 69
   presence of god in human form, 67–68
   specific god-forms, 68
   stereotypical role, 66
   sybil, 66–67
   transition from warrior to, 69
   true prophet, 69
   Underworld or Divine, 67
psychic properties or energies, 115
psychological archetypes, 4. *See also* god-within/-without
psychology, xxix
   alternative therapies, xxx
   problems of, xxix
   and spiritual traditions, xxix–xxxi
   and the gods, 4
Psychology and Spiritual Traditions, xxix

reading aloud, 111. *See also* visualizing transformation
rebirthing, xxx
religious meditation traditions, 100
revival of Goddess awareness, 26. *See also* men and the goddess
Right Hand and Left Hand interchange, 77–78
romantic escapism, 61
Room with Four Doors, 125–127, 129–130
   building the room, 126–128
   Doors and Mirror, 129
   encountering Five Branches, 130–133
   encountering poet, 133–134
   encountering priest, 135
   encountering prophet, 134
   Pentagonal Room, 131
   Presence of the Inner Warrior, 132
   Sacred Space, 128
   three emblems, 130
   12-week cycle, 126
   warrior, 130–132
   Warrior Departure, 132–133

Sacred. *See also* King within; Room with Four Doors; warrior
   Directions, 79
   King, 72
   Kingship, 88–93
   Space, 128
science and magic, 113. *See also* magic gods and visions

Scottish Schathach, 75
Sea Priestess, The, 23
security in outer forms, 102
See, Sense, and Feel method, 161–162
self transformation, spiritual methods of, 98
Seven Directions, 83–84
sexual. *See also* men and the goddess; polarity and sexuality
    energies, 106
    initiation, 44–46
    magic, 24
sexuality, 43. *See also* polarity and sexuality
    and death, 82
shadow, xxiv
shape, 82–83
short time scale, 139–140
Silence, 157–159
simple group method, 155–156
skills and crafts, 61–63. *See also* Five Branches
sleeping king, 137. *See also* King
    cycle of visions and encounters, 137–138
    Three Thresholds, 138
    12-week cycle, 137
    and wounded king, 138–139
sons of divine beings, 76–77. *See also* warrior
South, 84
specific god-forms, 68
spiritual
    balance, 23–24
    evolution, xxiii–xxiv
    meditation traditions, 100
    methods of self transformation, 98
    teachers for women, xxvii
    tradition, 114
Stillness. *See* Silence
strength and falling towers, 106–109. *See also* visualizing transformation
superior male concepts, xxii
super-males, 35. *See also* teachers and pupils

sword Excalibur, 77
sybil, 66–67. *See also* prophet

Tantra, 24
Tarot, 80, 108
    decks, 50
teacher, personal, 29–33. *See also* teachers and pupils
teachers and pupils, 29
    "appearing as male figures", 35
    concept of the all-male Master, 40
    cults and movements, 39
    Eastern religions, 40–41
    Hidden Masters, 38–41
    identifying inner-world teachers, 35–38
    Mantle, 33
    Masters, the, 29
    Merlin, 37
    metaphysical teachers, 33–34
    money, 30, 40
    New Age Hidden Masters, 41
    personal teacher/mentor/guru, 29–33
    relationship between pupil and teacher, 31–32
    skills, 30
    super-males, 35
    traditional teacher–pupil initiatory systems, 32–33
    working with inner-world teachers, 33–35
teaching, xxix
    crude and cruel, xxvii
    imposition of will, xxviii
    non-sentimental, xxvii
    spiritual teachers for women, xxvii
teaching methods, crude and cruel, xxvii
temple sexuality, 44. *See also* polarity and sexuality
Theosophical Society, xxi, 39
    Masters, xxii
    Women's Mysteries, xxi
three emblems, 130. *See also* Room with Four Doors

INDEX

Three Faces, The, 14–15
Three Thresholds, 125
   Pentagonal Room, 131
   sleeping king, 138
traditional teacher–pupil initiatory systems, 32–33. *See also* teachers and pupils
transcendence through celibacy, 24–25. *See also* men and the goddess
transformation, spiritual methods of self, 98
Tree of Life, The, 7, 9–10, 117–118. *See also* god-within/-without; magic gods and visions
   god-forms upon, 121
12-week cycle, 126–127. *See also* Room with Four Doors
12-week working timetable, 139

Underworld, 67. *See also* prophet
universal God, 116
Unknown, 82

visionaries, 68. *See also* prophet
visionary practice, 101. *See also* visualizing transformation
visions and encounters, 137–138
visualization, 161. *See also* Guardian; magic gods and visions; visualizing transformation
   conscious, 103–105
   of deities, 114
   wish-fulfilling visualization, 101
visualizing transformation, 97
   ancient visions and modern applications, 105–106
   basic methods of, 109–110
   breaking-down of patterns, 107
   concentrated image-making, 105
   conscious visualization, 103–105
   "discovery" of visualization, 103
   enhancing deep memory, 110
   envisioning future, 100–103
   esoteric traditions, 101
   exchange of energies, 100
   exercises, 97
   group work with reader, 111
   hidden traditions and training, 98
   imagination atrophies, 104–105
   individual power-centers, 99
   inner constructs, 107
   Inner Fire, 106
   magic, 107
   meditation, 100
   merits of visualizing methods, 110–111
   mythic lore, 105
   personal meditation and concentration, 99
   physical use of body, 99
   pre-recorded audio, 110–111
   reading aloud, 111
   security in outer forms, 102
   sexual energies, 106
   spiritual methods of self transformation, 98
   strength and falling towers, 106–109
   visionary practice, 101
   visualization, exercises, and energies, 99–100
   want and need, 102
   Western Esoteric Tradition, 97
   Wheel of Life, 100
   wish-fulfilling visualization, 101

warrior, 55, 69, 130–132. *See also* Five Branches
   ancient male aggression toward the Goddess, 75
   Classical goddesses, 75
   codes, 75
   dancer and, 65
   development of, 73
   ethical and spiritual values, 74
   false hero, 76
   Goddess, 141–142. *See also* Four Goddesses
   goddesses, 75
   and grail, 72–76
   Grail legends, 73, 77
   Grail, The, 73

great goddesses of sexuality and
    death, 75
as hero, 76–77
and ideal or model society, 71–72
King Arthur, 71, 77
magic of, 134
Presence of the Inner Warrior, 132
primal heroes, 76
religious conditioning, 75
Right Hand and Left Hand
    interchange, 77–78
Sacred King, 72
sons of divine beings, 76–77
strength and skill, 74
superficial or outermost level, 70
sword Excalibur, 77
training, 73
transition from, 69
Warrior Departure, 132–133
West, 85
Western Esoteric Tradition, 61, 97
Western magical arts, god in, 115
Wheel of Life, The, 7–8, 50, 83, 100.
    See also god-within/-without
White Goddess, The, xxv
will, imposition of, xxviii
wise elder, xxviii–xxix
wish-fulfilling visualization,
    101. *See also* visualizing
    transformation
Within, 86
Women's Mysteries, xxi
worker, 79
    Above, 85–86
    Below, 86
    East, 84
    fourfold Elemental pattern, 79
    human Elemental personae, 80
    link between sexuality and death,
        82
    losing power, 81–83
    male and female shape, 83
    North, 85
    primal universal patterns, 82
    Seven Directions, 83–84
    skills and crafts, 79–80
    South, 84
    Tarot, 80
    Unknown, 82
    West, 85
    Wheel of Life, 83
    Within, 86
wounded king, 138–139

www.ingramcontent.com/pod-product-compliance
Ingram Content Group UK Ltd.
Pitfield, Milton Keynes, MK11 3LW, UK
UKHW040840010725
460272UK00006B/120